56 CITADEL MINIATURES SHOWCASE

60 PAINTING MINIATURES

82 READYING FOR WAR

86 CORE RULES

STOP!
ASSEMBLE YOUR SPACE MARINE

To build your free Space Marine Intercessor follow the simple steps below. Once you're ready to paint him, check out the introduction to painting on page 60 and the step-by-step guide on page 74.

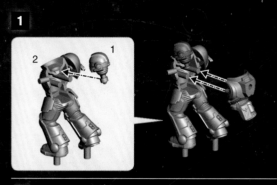

THE 41ST MILLENNIUM

The galaxy has seen ten thousand years of bitter war. Millennia ago the Emperor – the Master of Mankind and the most powerful human who has ever lived – sought to reunite his scattered race and forge an everlasting Imperium of Man. To this end he created the Space Marines, genetically enhanced warriors of unparalleled might. They were to be the Emperor's sword and shield, the ultimate weapon of his galactic reconquest. Under the command of the Primarchs, living demigods created from his own genetic material, the armies of the Emperor began their Great Crusade into the stars.

This dream of a glorious future perished in the fires of heresy and rebellion. The Dark Gods of Chaos, ancient beings of infinite malice formed from the accumulated passions and fears of mortal life, sought to consume the entire human race. They corrupted the Warmaster Horus, favoured son of the Emperor, and swayed fully half of the Space Marine Legions to their cause. Thus was the galaxy-wide atrocity of the Horus Heresy unleashed, and brother turned against brother in the most vicious conflict imaginable.

In a climactic battle upon the Imperial home world of Terra, the forces of Chaos were defeated at the last. This victory came at unthinkable cost, for though the Emperor felled Horus, he was mortally wounded by the Warmaster's hand. To this day his shrivelled carcass resides upon the Throne of Terra, its flesh writhing with power from the Dark Age of Technology. A thousand souls are sacrificed every day so that he may never truly die.

The Imperium of Man, once a promise of a glorious future for Humanity, is now a bloated realm ruled by corruption, fear and ignorance. The Emperor's loyal Primarchs were killed or disappeared over the centuries, and its billions-strong armies are the only shield against an onslaught of foes too numerous to count. Set against them are foul legions sworn to Chaos, led by the Heretic Astartes, those traitorous renegade Space Marines still fighting their Long War against the Imperium. Xenos hordes slaughter their way ever closer towards Holy Terra, while others sow insidious conspiracies amongst the populace of teeming hive worlds, which drown entire sectors of space in internecine bloodshed. There is no place in the galaxy for hope or mercy. Across the vastness of space there is only war, and the echoing laughter of thirsting gods.

DARK IMPERIUM

At the turn of the 41st Millennium the galaxy was torn apart by the greatest warp rift it had ever seen. Known as the Cicatrix Maledictum, the Great Rift, and by countless other names, this galaxy-spanning accumulation of warp storms allowed hordes of the hungry daemonic essences that dwell within the depths of the immaterium to pour into realspace and sate their foul appetites.

It was Abaddon the Despoiler – greatest mortal champion of the Chaos Gods – who sowed the seeds of this nightmare. After centuries of strategy and countless acts of atrocity, Abaddon brought ruin to the fortress world of Cadia, and shattered the mysterious, geometric pylon structures that dotted its surface. In doing so he tore the sutures from a wound which bisected the galaxy. The light of the Astronomican – the

psychic beacon which allows for communication and travel across the vast realm of the Imperium – was smothered, leaving entire planetary sectors isolated, and shrouding all in darkness and fear.

Yet in this time of utmost despair, the faintest spark of hope was kindled. From within the ranks of the alien Aeldari rose followers of the nascent

god of the dead, Ynnead. Obeying the will of their deity, these Ynnari enacted one last desperate gambit. Joining forces with a band of champions from the Imperium, they fought their way past the assembled forces of Chaos to reach Ultramar, domain of the Ultramarines.

Upon the hallowed ground of Macragge a ritual was performed. Roboute Guilliman, Primarch of the Ultramarines and the Avenging Son of the Emperor of Mankind, was reborn. Even as the forces of Chaos swarmed across the Imperium, Guilliman sallied forth upon a new crusade, striking back against those who would despoil his father's domain.

The Imperium is engulfed in total war. Agri world and hive planet alike must take up arms, for nowhere is safe from the depredations of Chaos. Xenos races plot their own ascension in the midst of this looming apocalypse. The warlike Orks gather for the greatest Waaagh! the galaxy has ever seen. Necron tomb worlds stir, ranks of pitiless androids waking from millennia of slumber to serve their cruel masters. The T'au plan new expansions of their burgeoning empire, and Tyranid hive fleets drift ever closer to the galactic core, drawn onwards by an insatiable hunger.

A new era of war has dawned. If there is a future at all for Humanity, it is one of unimaginable strife.

The Space Marines are the Imperium's best chance of survival in a hostile galaxy. Each is the product of arcane science and relentless training, leaving them stronger, taller and more resilient than those they fight for.

SPACE MARINES

Space Marines are genetically engineered super-human warriors. Armed and armoured with the best equipment the Imperium can provide, they are the Emperor's most elite fighting forces. To the Space Marines fall the most desperate and vital of the Imperium's battles, holding the line where all others have fallen, or striking like the Emperor's own blade to bring death to xenos warlords and daemonic abominations alike.

Space Marines are organised into Chapters, each consisting of one thousand battle-brothers and possessed of their own armouries, fighting vehicles, space fleets and towering fortress monasteries. Though there is less than one warrior of the Adeptus Astartes for every planet in the Imperium, it is a testament to their sheer might and heroism that this number is still sufficient to hurl back the enemies of Humanity upon every front.

Imperial Fists   Raven Guard   Salamanders

There are many Space Marine Chapters scattered across the Emperor's realm, each with its own warrior traditions and particular areas of expertise. The Ultramarines, for example, are exemplary warriors and masterful strategists, while the Imperial Fists are stubborn and determined masters of siegecraft. The Raven Guard favour stealth and misdirection, the White Scars speed and shock assault, while the Salamanders and Iron Hands are masters of wielding flame and mighty war machines respectively. Some Chapters, such as the feral and heroic Space Wolves or the secretive Dark Angels, are stranger still, but all fight for the same goal – the ongoing survival of the Imperium of Man.

Not all of the Heretic Astartes hail from the original Traitor Legions that fought during the Horus Heresy. The long centuries since have seen many loyalist Space Marine Chapters fall to the corrupting sway of Chaos, brought low by pride, bitterness, or simple ill fortune.

LEGIONS OF CHAOS

As the favoured champions of the Chaos Gods, the Heretic Astartes are blessed with many gifts. They may have profane boons bestowed upon them which grant unnatural strength and resilience, or horrific weapon-mutations that can peel the flesh from a foe with sickening ease.

The warbands and Legions of the Heretic Astartes each fight in their own unique manner; the World Eaters, for example, are berserkers who worship Khorne, the Blood God, and fall upon their foes in a gore-splattered orgy of slaughter. The eldritch Sorcerers of the Thousand Sons are some of the most powerful psykers in the galaxy, capable of burning scores of warriors to ash with a single incantation. Meanwhile the Death Guard march on their foes as an implacable wall of bloated flesh and pock-marked armour, their droning prayers to the Plague God, Nurgle, drowned out by the roar of their guns.

All manner of hideous creatures dwell within the warp, a hellish, roiling dimension in which the greatest passions and fears of mortal creatures are given terrible form. Acts of monstrous atrocity or foul ritual can weaken the barriers between realms, unleashing the nightmare of a daemonic incursion into realspace. Led by horrifically powerful Greater Daemons and Daemon Princes – mortals who have been granted the gift of Daemonhood – these profane hosts fight

Each Daemon of Chaos is formed from a fragment of a Dark God's essence, and thus they embody the traits and passions of their masters; Khorne's Daemons are rage-filled slaughterers, who care for nothing beyond their next kill. Nurgle's children are implacable, and often possess a morbid sense of humour. Daemons of Slaanesh embody the Dark Prince's aesthetic beauty and boundless sadism, while Tzeentch's creations are ever-changing and maddening

'Show these mewling wretches the true depth of their ignorance. Tear down their idols, and feed their false priests to the flames. Death to the False Emperor!'

The Heretic Astartes are Humanity's greatest foes, traitorous Space Marines who have turned from the light of the Emperor and embraced the baleful glory of Chaos. Consumed with bitter hatred, these champions of ruin prey upon the Imperium they once swore to defend.

ARMIES OF THE IMPERIUM

The innumerable regiments of the Astra Militarum hail from all across the vast expanse of the Imperium. It is the armoured fist of Humanity, comprising vast formations of battle tanks, artillery pieces and wing upon wing of aircraft that pound all before them into dust with a apocalyptic barrage of heavy munitions. Advancing behind this slegdehammer blow come countless ranks of men and women armed with nothing more than trusty lasguns and an unshakeable faith in the God-Emperor of Mankind.

The Adeptus Mechanicus is an ancient organisation of Tech-Priests who venerate the Emperor in the form of the Omnissiah, the Machine God. They are a strange, dispassionate breed, obsessed with the acquisition of lost knowledge. The fume-choked forge worlds of the Adeptus Mechanicus pump out a constant flow of munitions, weapons and war machines for the armies of the Imperium.

The forces of the Tech-Priests comprise all manner of ancient, arcane technology; maniples of bionically enhanced Skitarii warriors, Dunecrawlers, robots, battle servitors and bizarre processions of Electro-Priests singing atonal, static-warped hymns of praise to the Machine God. These armies are sent forth to scour the galaxy for forgotten secrets, and will slaughter anything that stands in the way of their holy mission.

Crest of House Terryn

Forged in the factory-temples of the Adeptus Mechanicus and piloted by noble warriors hailing from proud bloodlines, the Imperial Knights are towering bipedal war machines that bristle with devastating weaponry. A single one of these monstrous walkers can turn the tide of battle, while an entire Household of Knights has the martial might and unendurable firepower to conquer entire worlds.

Hailing from the secretive Schola Progenium, the shock troops of the Militarum Tempestus are amongst the very finest soldiers that the Imperium has at its disposal. Trained and indoctrinated from birth to be ruthless and unflinchingly loyal killers, they storm into battle with hot-shot lasguns blazing, cutting down the foe with relentless skill and precision.

Hot-shot Lasgun

THE AELDARI

The Aeldari are an alien race that once ruled the galaxy. Technologically, militarily and intellectually the Aeldari are as far superior to Humanity as Humanity are to primitive simians. They possess weapons that can extinguish stars, they tread secret paths beyond the bounds of reality, and their towering psychic might allows them to read and weave the strands of fate itself. Yet for all this the Aeldari are but an echo, a faded, splintered remnant of their former glory. Their numbers dwindle by the decade, and their battle is now one of survival, not supremacy.

There are many factions within the Aeldari race, each with its own distinct culture, aesthetics and ways of making war. The craftworld warhosts, for example, follow focussed paths that allow them to specialise in different aspects of warfare. Travelling the galaxy in vast ships known as craftworlds, these Aeldari seek balance and control in all things, fighting a war wherever they must to turn fate in their favour and preserve their people from destruction.

The Ynnari, meanwhile, are a recently risen faction within Aeldari society. They worship Ynnead, the god of the dead, a burgeoning power within the Aeldari pantheon. Through the leadership of Ynnead's high priestess, Yvraine, and other champions, the Ynnari use the souls of the slain to empower themselves in battle. The Ynnari believe themselves to be the saviours of their entire race, but there are those who fear they are no less than the final doom of the Aeldari made manifest.

Other Aeldari factions exist whose only goal is to win the endless war against the Chaos God Slaanesh, she who is the nemesis of the Aeldari race. The Harlequins are mysterious worshippers of the Laughing God, Cegorach. These acrobatic warrior-performers employ breath-taking speed and skill when acting out ritual tales for their kin, and these talents find even more use when the Harlequins fall upon their foes on the battlefield.

The Drukhari are very different from their craftworlder kin. Sallying out on piratical raids from the Dark City, Commorragh, the Drukhari seek to inflict as much pain and misery upon their victims as they possibly can, for it is this that sustains their withered spirits through the long millennia. No act of depravity or cruelty is too great for the warrior Kabals, the gladiatorial Wych Cults or the flesh-twisting Haemonculus Covens, and they compete with each other to win the greatest prizes.

ORKS

The belligerent and warlike Orks have been a blight on the galaxy since time immemorial. The entire culture of these brutish xenos is centred around warfare. They live for the exhilaration of a good fight, the deafening thunder of gunfire, and the rush of hurtling into battle in speeding, ramshackle fighting vehicles. When gathered into their billions-strong hordes they can spell the doom of entire space sectors.

Ork technology is scrapped together from whatever raw materials are found near to hand, and as a result it is ramshackle, crude and often dangerously unreliable. Despite, or perhaps because of this unpredictability, it can also be utterly deadly – to the wielder as well as his target.

When Orks gather in sufficient numbers, flocking to the banners of the hulking brutes known as Warbosses, they will embark upon a Waaagh! - an unstoppable crusade driven by unquenchable battle-lust. Vast hordes of Orks sweep across planet after planet, crushing all before them in a deafening, smoke-belching tide of clanking war machines. All semblance or order and civilisation is torn down, shattered and burned, and amidst the ashes the Orks gather around their towering war effigies, bellowing praises to the monstrous gods they call Gork and Mork.

ARMIES OF THE 41ST MILLENNIUM

THE XENOS THREAT

T'AU EMPIRE

The T'au Empire is a dynamic rising power in the galaxy, an expansionist, caste-based technocracy built upon the philosophical ideal of the Greater Good. The T'au are determined to enforce this vision of galactic unity by any means, and many uncooperative civilisations have been pacified by the application of their advanced weaponry and considerable military presence. The T'au Fire caste train from birth in the arts of war, and wield high-tech plasma weaponry, armoured battlesuits and countless other cutting-edge technologies to ensure their armies are ready to face any resistance.

The mysterious beings known as Ethereals dominate T'au society. These spiritual leaders command absolute respect and authority amongst their people, and inspire in them a fanatical zeal. T'au Fire Warriors will stand defiant in the face of impossible odds should an Ethereal command it, gladly offering their lives in service to the Greater Good.

NECRONS

The Necrons are a race of sentient androids who long ago traded away their souls for the gift of immortality. For millennia beyond counting they have slumbered within their tomb worlds, sprawling crypt-fortresses that house billions-strong armies and ranks of deadly war machines. With every passing year more Necrons arise from this long stasis, and as they awaken so they begin the process of reforging their dynastic empires, which once ruled the galaxy with an iron fist.

To earn their immortality, the Necrontyr sacrificed their very flesh, replacing it with living metal. This renders even the lowliest Necron warrior incredibly resilient and difficult to kill. Yet such strength comes at a terrible cost. The majority of the Necron race are little more than near-mindless thralls, enslaved to the will of cruel Overlords – driven insane by millennia of dreaming stasis – who are still determined to see the Necron Empire rise once more.

The Tyranids are utterly alien. They employ no mechanical technology whatsoever, instead spawning living creatures to fulfil every role and task. Whether it be their countless weapon-beasts, the bone blades and bile-spraying guns they wield, or even the vast, arthropoidal space ships that carry them through the void, all Tyranids are living creatures and all are controlled by the vast gestalt consciousness known as the Hive Mind. It is this godlike sentience that drives the hive fleets ever onward, and coordinates their attacks with eerie precision.

TYRANIDS AND GENESTEALER CULTS

From the endless darkness of the galactic void, a terrible threat descends upon the worlds of Mankind and their enemies alike. Filled with an endless, monstrous hunger, the swarming beasts of the Tyranid hive fleets devour all life in their path and leave nothing behind themselves but airless worlds of dead and shattered stone.

The Imperium has faced many Tyranid hive fleets over recent centuries, each with its own distinctive traits and tactics. Hive Fleet Behemoth struck the eastern fringe like a battering ram, a single, unified horde that almost wiped out the Ultramarines Chapter before it was finally destroyed. Hive Fleet Kraken surged into Imperial space as many, splintered hive fleets, while Leviathan pushed up from below the galactic plane, and seemed more adaptable and numerous than any hive fleet that had come before it. With every fresh invasion, the Tyranids become ever more deadly to face, and ever more costly to stop.

On many Human worlds, insidious cults have taken hold. Spread like a sickness by the infiltrating Tyranid creatures known as Genestealers, these cults venerate the hive fleets as divine star gods. Driven by a psychic imperative, the Genestealer Cults subvert and undermine Imperial society, all the while beaming out a psychic beacon that draws the hive fleets down upon them. When the Tyranids at last darken the skies, the Cults rise up to overthrow their oppressors and welcome their divine saviours with open arms.

COLLECTING CITADEL MINIATURES

The galaxy of the 41st Millennium is a place of mighty champions, foul heretics and bloodthirsty alien monstrosities. It is a galaxy filled with both grandeur and horror, gothic beauty and foul corruption. These rich characters and themes are brought to life in the form of beautifully rendered Citadel Miniatures, from the massed ranks of foot-slogging Astra Militarum troops to the regal majesty of an Aeldari Wraithlord.

One of the greatest joys for any hobbyist is to see their freshly assembled army take to the gaming table, and compete with their friends' collections in a bout of all-out war. Many players connect with a particular faction or race within the Warhammer 40,000 setting, and enjoy the satisfying feeling of building up a personalised force packed with colourful characters and arcane war machines. Others relish the act of building and painting itself, and create incredible battlefield dioramas to showcase their lovingly assembled miniatures. There is no right or wrong way to enjoy the Warhammer 40,000 hobby, and for many enthusiasts it is the combined alchemy of all these different factors that makes collecting so enjoyable.

Roboute Guilliman, the resurrected Primarch of the Ultramarines Chapter. There is no greater hero in the Imperium of Man.

While building a large collection can feel intimidating at first, it's important to remember that you don't have to assemble everything at once! Games Workshop offers a range of Start Collecting! boxes that feature a great selection of units for each army, an excellent starting point for any budding hobbyist. Once you have a solid core to your collection built and painted, you can start planning what to add to it next.

CODEXES

Games Workshop publishes a range of codexes to accompany the playable armies available in Warhammer 40,000. Each codex is an indispensable guide to that faction, providing an in-depth look at their background and history, their iconography and colour schemes, as well as a comprehensive set of rules for forging your collection of Citadel Miniatures into a devastating tabletop army, ready to face your opponents upon the field of battle.

WARHAMMER 40,000

CODEX ADEPTUS ASTARTES
GREY KNIGHTS

WHERE TO START?

With over thirty years of fantastic publications behind it, the Warhammer 40,000 setting possesses a wealth of depth and excitement to inspire your collection. Many people choose to collect an army based upon its background, choosing a specific story, character, campaign or named army and recreating them upon the tabletop down to the last detail. Others use the narrative as their starting point and delight in weaving their own characters and factions into the setting, inventing their own colour schemes and heroic warriors in order to truly make their collection their own. Either route is an exciting gateway into the Warhammer 40,000 hobby.

Many collections are inspired by the ancient enmities of the Warhammer 40,000 galaxy.

COLLECTING TO PLAY

Once you dive into the Warhammer 40,000 tabletop wargame, you'll soon discover which experiences and styles of play you enjoy the most, and start adding to your collection accordingly. There are datasheets available for every miniature that Games Workshop releases, which will give you an idea of how each unit works on the battlefield. While it's important to remember that gaming should be fun for everyone, it's fun to identify your army's strengths, and add models together that complement each other particularly well. This can be a great hook to drive your collection, though you can have just as much fun with a force filled with units that appeal to you personally.

As a collection grows, you have even more choice when picking an army for games.

COLLECTING TO DISPLAY

Every single Citadel Miniature is full of character and packed with detail. There are also an incredible amount to choose from, with more being released all the time. For many hobbyists, it's often a case of picking up whatever draws their attention. Some prefer to collect single models, often heroes and champions, upon which they can lavish their utmost attention. Others are particularly devoted to certain factions or unit types – the implacable, pox-ridden legions of the Death Guard, for example, or the monstrous bio-organisms of the Tyranids. Over time your painting skills will improve and you might want to take on ever greater and more challenging projects.

A beautifully-realised collection like this is well worthy of a place in a display cabinet.

A Captain leads his troops into battle, power sword raised defiantly at the foe.

COLLECTION
ULTRAMARINES

Noble warriors and peerless strategists, the Ultramarines are the epitome of what it means to be a Space Marine. Led by their resurrected Primarch Roboute Guilliman, they will fight to the last to preserve the Imperium of Man.

There are few more striking sights upon the tabletop than a fully assembled Space Marine strike force. Each miniature in this range radiates martial authority and sheer might, from the clean, imposing lines of their power armour to the rugged lethality of their bolters and plasma incinerators. With dynamic, poseable stances and a multitude of weapon options, you can really bring each individual model to life, while never losing the sense of visual cohesion that ties the entire army together.

This force was chosen with the intent of showing off the fast-moving, hard-hitting Space Marines upon the tabletop battlefield. Inspired by the jaw-dropping Roboute Guilliman miniature, and by the numerous tales of heroism in *Codex: Space Marines*, it's built around the models found in the Know No Fear starter set, painted in the blue of the Ultramarines. This specific collection displays the red shoulder-guard trim of the Ultramarines' 3rd Company; the Space Marine codex includes a great range of different companies and colour schemes you can apply to your own models.

The Space Marines are an incredibly versatile army, providing a collector with a wide range of exciting miniatures to choose from. Whether you prefer heavy firepower, fast-moving assault troopers, armoured battle tanks, mighty heroes or any other strategic permutation, the Space Marines have units to meet your needs.

This collection is a strategically flexible force, capable of handling whatever situation arises while also looking fantastic and feeling exciting and enjoyable to play with. The starter set includes a hard core of Primaris Space Marines, to which we added a Tactical Squad and a squad of elite Terminators. A Terminator Librarian joined our Captain, ready to aid the cause with his prodigious psychic might. Finally, we added armoured and aerial support in the form of a Repulsor tank and a Stormtalon Gunship. With these armoured assets added to the ranks, the army is ready for war!

If you're hungry to start your own Space Marine collection, check out the Painting section on page 60 – there's a simple guide to painting your first Intercessors and Reivers, and a detailed guide to the Citadel Painting System.

The Lord of Contagion is bedecked in corrupted Terminator plate, and wields an enormous plaguereaper covered in rust and toxins.

This Daemon Prince has been modelled and painted to represent its allegiance to the Plague God, Nurgle.

SERVANTS OF NURGLE

Nurgle is the Lord of Decay, the Chaos God of disease and pestilence. His daemonic and mortal legions alike are riddled with his bountiful gifts, including plagues and mutations that grant them hideous resilience.

For those who enjoy painting putrescent flesh, rusting blades and other grisly and disgusting marks of corruption, the forces of Nurgle are the perfect army to collect. From the bizarre mutations of the Plague Marines to the gleeful mischievousness of bounding Nurglings, each model dedicated to the Plague God is full of vivid character and enjoyably disgusting flourishes. You can really express yourself through painting and assembling your Nurgle-themed collection, and experiment with different paints and techniques to convey the glorious bounty of Nurgle's gifts.

This force evokes the narrative of an unholy alliance of servants of Nurgle, as it includes both Death Guard and Nurgle Daemons. The army is roughly split into two sections – the Death Guard are led by a deadly Lord of Contagion, while the daemonic infantry are captained by a Daemon Prince of Nurgle. The ability to combine daemonic troops with Heretic Astartes opens up many possibilities when collecting and assembling an army, and provides impressive visual variety and adaptability on the battlefield.

Inspired by the grotesque Daemon Engines of the Death Guard, we couldn't resist including a couple of these awesome models in the mortal portion of the force. The models from the starter set helped with this goal; not only does it include a powerful leader and solid base of infantry models in the Lord of Contagion, Plague Marines and Poxwalkers, but it also provides a Foetid Bloat-drone. To this, we added the armoured might of a Plagueburst Crawler, whose potent firepower would be the bane of its enemies.

The Daemon force was then chosen to complement this armoured core – shambling hordes of Plaguebearers and Nurglings boost both the army's numbers and its survivability. These are backed up by airborne Plague Drones and led by a Daemon Prince whose strength, resilience and psychic abilities will render the army even more powerful on the tabletop.

If you're inspired to create your own Death Guard collection, check out the Painting section on page 60 – as well as covering all the techniques you'll need, there's a handy guide to painting Plague Marines and Poxwalkers.

COLLECTION
AELDARI WARHOST

The Aeldari are one of the most ancient and powerful xenos species in the galaxy. Their fractured society is divided into many different factions, each with their own strengths and specialisms. This collection combines several of these factions into one potent whole.

A Shadowseer leads the contingent of Harlequins, an enigmatic psyker whose hallucinatory magic drives her enemies to insanity.

This collection showcases the sheer variety of the Aeldari range – although they can each field their own armies, this collection combines the deadly elegance of the Craftworld Aeldari, the barbed menace of the Drukhari and the kaleidoscopic spectacle of the enigmatic Harlequins into one exciting whole.

The lynchpin of this collection is the famed Farseer, Eldrad Ulthran. Not only is this model stunning in its own right – an enjoyable challenge for any painter – but Eldrad is infamous for using his powers of foresight, diplomacy and manipulation to forge allegiances between his scattered peoples. With Eldrad as the centrepiece and narrative link, we combed through the Aeldari ranges for miniatures that would complement each other visually and on the gaming table.

Its heart is a solid core of Craftworld Aeldari infantry – the Guardians and Wraithguard – supported by a towering Wraithlord, multiple grav-tanks, and a swift squadron of Windrider jetbikes.

To these are added a light, swift complement of Drukhari centred around a skimming Raider transport ridden by a black-hearted Archon and his Kabalite Warriors. Flanking this piratical skiff are two squadrons of Reaver jetbikes to further enhance the force's speed and firepower.

One element of Aeldari society is famous for providing a link between the disperate Craftworlders and Drukhari – the Harlequins. We've chosen a lithe and deadly Harlequin Troupe to represent this faction, led into battle by a leering Death Jester and a psychically gifted Shadowseer. There are already plenty of jetbike-mounted troops in the army, but we could have added even more in the form of Harlequin Skyweavers or a graceful Starweaver transport – these would also be great additions to this collection.

United by their graceful aesthetics, distinguished by contrasting yet complementary colour schemes, the army looks amazing, evokes an exciting narrative, and would be an exciting and powerful force to field in battle. It's ready to be deployed upon the tabletop, there to fight for the Aeldari cause.

The Warlock Skyrunner is a highly mobile warrior and psyker, able to respond to emerging battlefield threats in the blink of an eye.

PLAYING GAMES

INTO THE FRAY

Once your army is assembled and painted, it's ready to take to the grim battlefields of the 41st Millennium. There is no greater feeling for many hobbyists than to see the miniatures they have worked so hard on come to life on the gaming table, and with Games Workshop's Warhammer 40,000 rules system – designed to be fun and immersive, yet incredibly easy to get to grips with – you have a framework that allows you to forge countless new legends in the grim darkness of the far future. Perhaps you'll take on the role of the courageous Space Marines, making a heroic last stand against impossible odds. You might wish to play as the ambitious T'au Empire, flexible warriors equipped with technologically advanced weaponry and agile battlesuits. Or maybe you'd prefer to embrace your inner megalomaniac and watch the galaxy burn, crushing everything before you with Chaos-warped tanks and Daemon Engines. Whatever game you want to play – grand, apocalyptic showdown or small-scale skirmish – the Warhammer 40,000 rules give you a framework to help you realise it.

Every player approaches games in their own way, but most games fall into one of the three broad gaming styles on the right, each of which offers a uniquely rewarding experience; open play, narrative play and matched play.

TOOLS OF WAR

To play the Warhammer 40,000 tabletop wargame, you'll need several six-sided dice – also referred to as D6 – as well as a range finder or ruler for measuring distances. Games Workshop offers thematic dice and tape measures as well as a variety of other accessories for enhancing your gaming experience, such as reference datacards for your army.

Here, Steve and Natalie are using their Death Guard and Ultramarines in battle. A game this size can last a couple of hours.

> 'For many gaming enthusiasts, it's the challenge of taking on other players that truly appeals.'

OPEN PLAY

Open play is the easiest way to begin playing games, because all you need is to get some models together and start rolling dice. There's no need to plan your army in advance – instead you and your opponent simply choose whichever models you want to play with, set them up and start gaming. This is a good way of trying out unusual army combinations, and perfect for beginners who may not have yet assembled a large and varied army. You can supplement this freeform fun by sprinkling in a few rules or guidelines from various Warhammer 40,000 supplements, or even create your own scenarios and unique challenges.

NARRATIVE PLAY

The Warhammer 40,000 universe is filled with mighty heroes, diabolical villains and tales of great courage and despicable brutality. Narrative play is all about tying the game you're playing on the table into that overarching narrative, helping you make those legendary sagas your own. Before you start a narrative game, the players should get together and think about the story they want to tell, and the motivations and objectives of their armies. Each player should choose a force that fits the tale being told, and a few house rules and bespoke terrain pieces really help bring the story to life. Narrative play is an incredibly fun and engaging way to immerse yourself in this uniquely dark and thrilling setting.

MATCHED PLAY

For many gaming enthusiasts, it's the challenge of taking on other players that truly appeals. Matched play is focussed around providing a level playing field, and to that end it involves ensuring that each force at the table features a roughly equivalent strength – this is as simple as adding up the points costs of each model and weapon, and setting an upper limit that both players must adhere to. This allows you to really test your strategic mind against your opponent. If you really get a taste for competitive play, there are lots of like-minded wargamers out there who run tournaments using matched play rules.

BATTLE FOR THE BUNKER

For many Warhammer 40,000 collectors, taking their lovingly assembled and painted Citadel Miniatures to the tabletop for a bout of wargaming is the heart of their hobby. The best way to discover just how much fun this can be is to see a game being played, from setup and deployment to the dramatic closing stages. The following battle report sees Andy's strike force of noble Ultramarines battling the horrific might of Nick's combined Death Guard and Nurgle Daemons army.

The first stage of any game is to determine the mission and set up the relevant terrain. For this match-up, Andy and Nick have decided to keep things simple. They've designated a single objective to contest – a statue in the centre of the map that cunningly conceals a vital command bunker. They decide that the planet upon which they are fighting has been wracked by virus bombardments from Chaos forces, and the majority of its standing armies have been driven deep underground in an attempt to escape the toxic fumes. An important Astra Militarum general is hiding within this particular bunker, and both an Ultramarines strike force and a combined Death Guard and Daemon host have their sights upon him. The chosen of Nurgle intend to sacrifice the general in a blasphemous

ritual to the God of Decay, while the Space Marines are here to rescue the beleaguered general before the Heretic Astartes can lay claim to him.

With the background for their battle decided upon, Andy and Nick assemble a fitting battlefield using various pieces of Citadel terrain. In the top right corner of the table there is a half-destroyed supply depot, littered with crates and barrels. In the bottom left they have fashioned a shattered manufactorum structure, adding to the war-torn industrial feel of the battlefield. In order to ensure a level playing field, each player has a roughly equal amount of cover on his side of the table, while in the middle of the board there's plenty of open space for tanks and other vehicles to manoeuvre.

Finally, Andy and Nick assign psychic powers to their psyker units – the Nurgle Daemon Prince for Nick, and the Terminator Librarian for Andy.

Both of these characters know the deadly *Smite* power, and they can also both choose a single power from their faction's psychic disciplines. Nick's Daemon Prince gets *Warptime*, which allows him to spirit his allies into battle with unnatural speed. Andy chooses *Might of Heroes* for his Librarian, a power that renders its target unit stronger, faster and even harder to kill.

Their mission chosen and their armies arrayed, it's time to find out who will win the day – Andy's heroic Ultramarines or Nick's putrid and hideously resilient legions of Nurgle!

Captain Narvis blocked the creature's awkward swing and struck out with his boltstorm gauntlet, shattering the abomination's skull in a spray of foul-smelling viscera.

'Captain!' shouted Sergeant Hadron. The Space Marine's helm was cracked at the jaw where a bolt round had skipped off the ceramite plate. 'Traitor Marines, advancing from the ruins.'

His words were punctuated by a searing blast of plasma that roared past Narvis and blasted Brother Pyrol off his feet. The Captain turned and saw them. Clad in rusted, pus-slick armour the colour of a spoiled wound, they came on. Plague Marines.

'Rally to me, brothers,' he shouted. 'And let us deliver the Emperor's justice to these wretched heretics!'

DEPLOYMENT

Before the battle begins in earnest, both players roll off to find out who begins setting up their units first. The mission they've come up with has the battlefield split in half length-wise, and so Andy and Nick deploy their armies along opposite edges of the board, each placing one unit at a time.

A

D

PRIMARY OBJECTIVE

B

ULTRAMARINES

Andy's Ultramarines offer a versatile blend of rugged fortitude and breathtaking firepower. The core of his force consists of a unit of ten Tactical Marines and an Intercessor Squad. Deadly warriors who can unleash a furious storm of bolt rounds with their rapid-firing bolt rifles, Andy's Intercessors are the perfect counter to Nick's shambling hordes of Nurgle Daemons and Poxwalkers. They begin the game inside a Repulsor tank – armed with lascannons, a heavy onslaught gatling cannon and other spectacularly lethal weapons, the Repulsor is a truly fearsome force upon the battlefield. Leading Andy's infantry is a Captain in Mk X Gravis armour, a devastatingly effective melee champion who can inspire his men to greater deeds in the midst of battle. Andy has also included a plasma-spitting Hellblaster Squad and a swift Stormtalon Gunship to dominate the skies above the battlefield.

B

DEATH GUARD

Nick has gone for numbers with his army list, trusting in the horrific fortitude of Nurgle Daemons and heretic Death Guard. He has a unit of twenty Poxwalkers, shambling melee troops who do a great job of soaking up enemy bolt rounds. They are lead by a Lord of Contagion, a mighty warrior in Terminator armour who carries an enormous Plaguereaper smeared in deadly toxins. Nick's five Plague Marines will start the game in a Chaos Rhino transport, while a Plagueburst Crawler and a Foetid Bloat-drone provide devastating fire support. Battling alongside the Heretic Astartes is a Nurgle Daemon Prince, supported by several swarms of mischievous Nurglings, a unit of Plaguebearers and a pack of flying Plague Drones.

Andy opts for a defensive strategic position on the left flank, placing a squad of Hellblasters in a fortified tower **A** that gives them some nice cover and a good view of the battlefield. His Tactical Squad takes the right flank, and is supported by a Repulsor Tank **B** and its complement of Intercessors, as well as his Captain **C**. Soaring menacingly overhead is his Stormtalon Gunship, a flying unit that can cross the battlefield in a single turn. The rules for his Terminators and Librarian allow Andy to keep these models off the battlefield to begin with, which he does. They will be ready to teleport in wherever they are needed.

Nick decides that he's going to try to outflank Andy by sweeping half of his forces around the left flank. His Daemon Prince of Nurgle is in charge of this manoeuvre, and commands a unit of Plaguebearers and some Nurglings **D**. His Plagueburst Crawler starts towards the middle of the board, with his Chaos Rhino in tow bearing five Plague Marines **E**. His Foetid Bloat-drone lurks further over, dribbling unspeakable liquids from its plaguespitters. Last but most definitely not least, his Lord of Contagion comes stomping out of the destroyed supply yard on the right flank, a horde of repulsive Poxwalkers shambling before him **F**. Like Andy's Terminators, Nick's Plague Drones start the battle off the table, ready to be summoned forth from the warp when Nick needs them later in the battle.

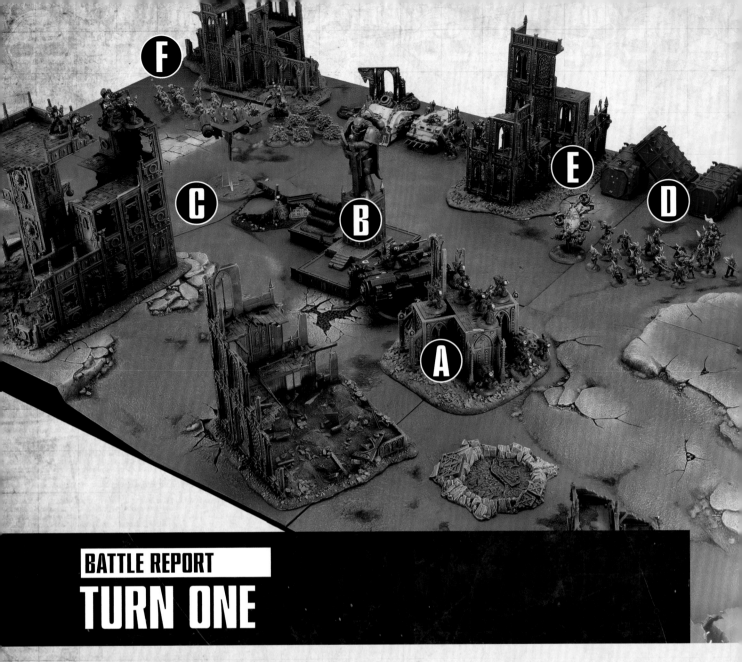

BATTLE REPORT
TURN ONE

Andy and Nick both roll a single dice to decide who takes the first turn of the game. Andy rolls highest, and therefore gets to choose who begins the game. The ability to move and strike first suits the mobile, aggressive army that he commands, and so he decides to start things off, and wastes no time in moving to secure key locations on the battlefield. Recognizing that he needs to thin the ranks of the pus-dripping Poxwalkers as soon as possible, he chooses to Advance (or run) his Tactical Squad into a fortified position to the right of the command bunker **A**.

Advancing means that this unit can't shoot or charge this round, but Andy is gambling that it will take time for the shambling ranks of Poxwalkers – who lack any ranged weapons of their own – to engage his troops. His Repulsor advances forward and opens fire on the Foetid Bloat-drone **B**, dealing a solid hit, and his Stormtalon zooms across the battlefield **C** to riddle the flanking Plaguebearers with cannon rounds. A swirling cloud of flies masks the majority of the Daemons from harm, but several explode in bursts of putrescent fluid.

In his first turn, Nick advances his Poxwalkers slowly forward **D**, using them to screen his Lord of Contagion – enemy models can't shoot at an Character model unless they're the closest model to them. His Foetid Bloat-drone moves up alongside the Poxwalkers **E** and showers Andy's Tactical Squad with a blast of putrid, flesh-rotting liquids from its plaguespitter cannons. These weapons automatically hit, representing the horrific cascade that they spew forth, but fortunately the Space Marines can take cover amongst the ruins, giving them a better chance of surviving the attack. Three Tactical Marines go down, and a further three fall to an accurate blast from Nick's Plagueburst Crawler.

Meanwhile, his daemonic forces lurch forwards on the right **F**. Plaguebearers are not particularly swift, but during the Psychic phase of his turn Nick's Daemon Prince casts *Warptime* on the shambling Daemons. They flicker in and out of reality, drawing nearer to their quarry with every blink. Essentially, this sneaky manoeuvre gives the Plaguebearers an extra move action, allowing them to close in on Andy's squad of Hellblasters.

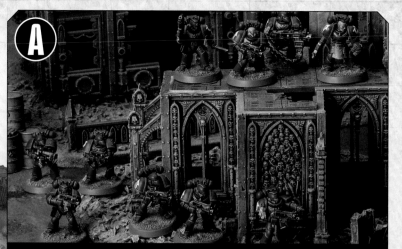

A Tactical Marines take cover in some shattered ruins. This makes them harder to hit, and gives them a fine view of the battlefield.

B The Repulsor.is a lethal weapons platform, but it can also transport squads of warriors into battle.

C The Stormtalon can switch from supersonic to hover mode, sacrificing speed for manoeuvrability.

D Poxwalkers make for an excellent shield against ranged fire, with the added bonus that they can replenish their numbers by killing foes in close combat.

As transports from both armies move to contest the centre of the battlefield, the stage is set for brutal close combat in the next turn.

E The Foetid Bloat-drone is a swift and lethal anti-infantry vehicle that can take incredible punishment.

F Nick's Plaguebearers and Nurglings are severely disadvantaged against Andy's Stormtalon Gunship, as they lack ranged attacks of any kind.

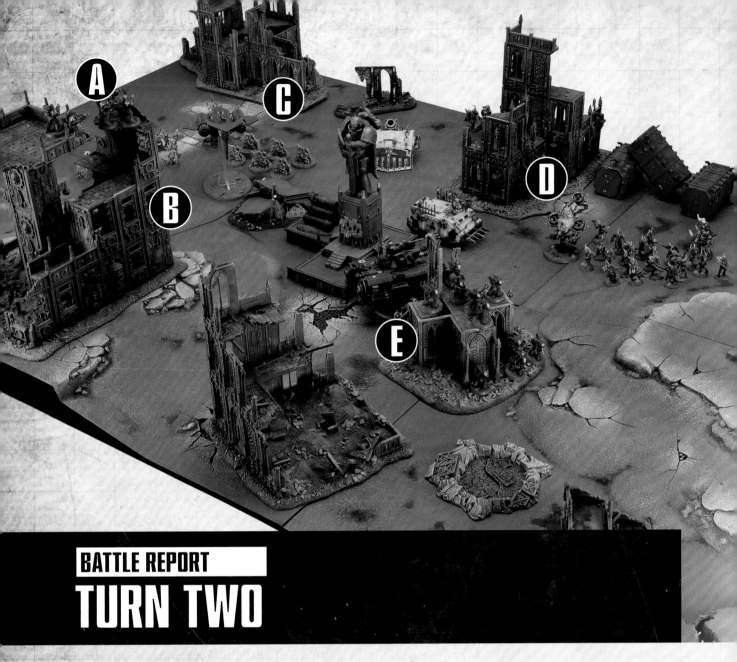

TURN TWO

The Ultramarines are known for their strategic brilliance, and at the end of Andy's Movement phase they prove that this accolade is well-earned. Reality twists and crackles as his squad of Terminators teleports in on the left flank, followed swiftly by a Librarian in Terminator armour Ⓐ. They arrive in perfect order, ready to encircle Nick's daemonic troops. To complete the trap, three Inceptors drop from the sky on their heavy jump packs, landing at the foot of the tower containing Andy's Hellblaster Squad Ⓑ. In a moment, the momentum of this portion of the battlefield has completely shifted.

With his Librarian in the field, Andy gets to act in the psychic phase for the first time. He can attempt to manifest two powers with his Librarian each turn, so he opts to kick things off with a damage-dealing *Smite* power aimed at the Daemon Prince of Nurgle. A sledgehammer of eldritch energy rushes towards the monstrous creature. Fortunately for Nick, he can attempt to shrug off this deadly strike with a Deny the Witch roll. He succeeds! Andy uses his second casting to bestow the strength-enhancing *Might of Heroes* on his Terminators, who are close enough to the Plaguebearers that they can attempt to charge into combat this turn. In the shooting phase Andy's Ultramarines pick off several Poxwalkers and badly damage the Foetid Bloat-drone. The Daemon Prince also takes a nasty five wounds from the hovering Stormtalon Ⓒ. Andy's psychically-enhanced Terminators attempt to charge the Plaguebearers, who they've already whittled down with their shooting. To do so, Andy rolls two dice. The number rolled represents how far in inches his unit

can charge. Unfortunately he rolls a total of three. The Plaguebearers are seven inches away, so the Terminators fail their charge attempt. Even worse for the Ultramarines, the Plaguebearers' special ability allows them to return from the dead thanks to the fickle powers of the warp. This isn't guaranteed, but with a lucky dice roll, Nick returns no less than six of the droning monsters to the battlefield!

It's Nick's turn, and his Lord of Contagion leads his Poxwalkers towards the Intercessors' defensive line Ⓓ, backed up by his Plague Marines, who disembark from their Chaos Rhino. The Daemon Prince leads the attack on the right flank, sending his Nurglings towards the Inceptors while his Plaguebearers turn and rush towards their Terminator assailants. Wary of the Stormtalon currently pouring fire

Terminators are the perfect shock troops. offering both deadly firepower and close combat expertise. Thanks to their ancient suits of armour, they are also very difficult to kill.

The Bloat-drone suffers several wounds, reducing its speed and weapon strength.

Inceptors' bulky jump packs allow them to crush foes when they charge into combat.

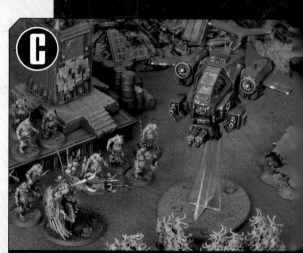

Designed for air-to-ground assaults, the Stormtalon Gunship gains a bonus to its attacks when performing strafing runs.

into his ranks, he also summons Nick's Plague Drones. A deafening buzzing fills the air as the daemonic fly-riders zoom towards the gunship. The Plague Marines and the Foetid Bloat-drone mow down two Intercessors and a Tactical Marine in the shooting phase, though the Bloat-drone is less effective now that it has lost so many wounds. In the charge phase, Nick sends it towards the Intercessor Squad regardless, recognizing that it's not going to last much longer. Defending units are granted an opportunity to fire at enemies who charge them Ⓔ – a special attack known as overwatch – though when they do this their shots only hit on rolls of a 6. Nevertheless, Andy's Intercessors rake the Bloat-drone with bolt rounds, and it explodes in a shower of pus and rusted metal shards, taking out an Intercessor and a Plague Marine as it does so.

Andy's Captain and Intercessor Squad disembark from the Repulsor, ready to unleash a fusillade of bolt rifle fire against anyone foolish enough to charge them.

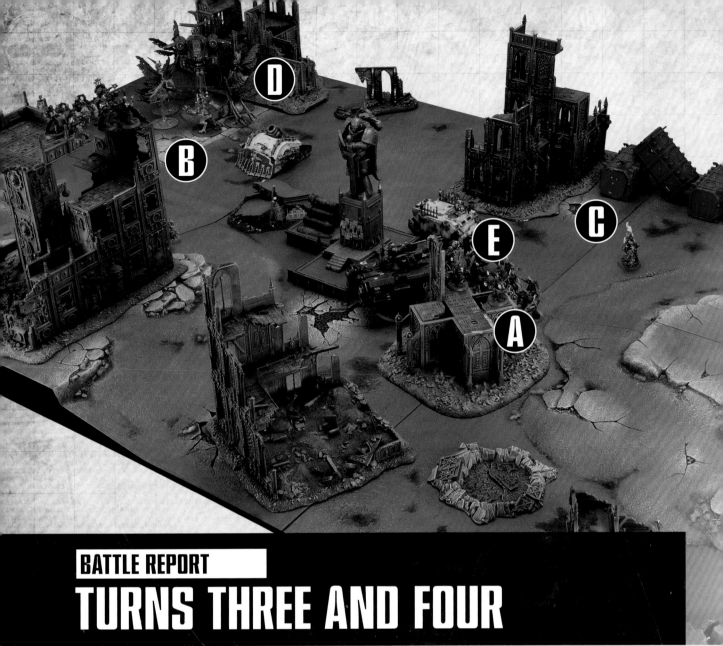

TURNS THREE AND FOUR

The battle rests upon a knife edge. Nick has numbers on his side, but so far Andy's Ultramarines have had the upper hand in close combat. His Captain in Gravis armour has already ripped apart two Plague Marines, and his hardy Intercessors – who can suffer two wounds each before they die – are proving immensely difficult to kill **A**.

Andy's Librarian prepares to take on the Daemon Prince, casting *Might of Heroes* upon himself to increase his power. He charges in and strikes the towering creature several times as they clash in the midst of the roiling battlefield **B**, badly hurting it but failing to score a lethal blow. Meanwhile, Andy's Captain finishes his impressive dismemberment of Nick's Plague Marines, cutting down the remaining three with his boltstorm gauntlet and power sword before they have a chance to land a blow on him.

Nick has taken some significant losses, but he has finally managed to get his Lord of Contagion into combat. Even worse for Andy, the warlord's Gift of Nurgle ability summons a pestilential aura of disease around him, a nasty ability that causes mortal wounds. Mortal wounds represent particularly horrific injuries that bypass armour entirely, and are a great way of dishing out damage to tough leaders, vehicles and monsters. This miasma of decay wounds the Captain and dissolves another Intercessor! The Lord of Contagion closes in on the bunker door, striding ominously through a field of corpses. The only thing standing in his way is Andy's heroic Captain, and the Nurgle warlord charges towards his foe with his Plaguereaper raised high **C**. He crashes into the Ultramarine, smashing through his Gravis armour and leaving the Captain

sorely wounded! Meanwhile, the Plague Drones swarm over the Stormtalon and bring it down, though the resulting crash wipes out another of their number **D**. Despite the Terminator Librarian's noble efforts, Nick's Daemon Prince viciously cuts him down with slashes from his Daemon sword.

In the shooting phase of Andy's fourth turn, the Daemon Prince finally falls to a punishing volley of bolt rounds from the Terminator Squad. It looks as though the left flank belongs to the Ultramarines, but the troops on that side of the battlefield will never reach the vital command bunker in time. If Andy's Captain can't hold back the Lord of Contagion and his remaining Poxwalkers, the battle is surely lost!

In front of the command bunker doors, the Captain and his Intercessor

The Captain's charismatic presence inspires nearby units from the same Chapter, improving their chances of hitting the foe.

The Librarian is no match for the Daemon Prince in a duel – unless he has enhanced his might with psychic powers.

The Plagueburst Crawler and the Repulsor tank meet on the battlefield, pummelling each other with heavy fire.

The Lord of Contagion's Terminator armour slows him down, but his Poxwalkers will keep the enemy busy until he enters the fray.

Sergeant face off against the remaining Poxwalkers and the Lord of Contagion. The Sergeant fights heroically, slicing the final Poxwalkers apart after they fail to land a blow **E**. The Chaos warlord slashes away with his Plaguereaper and scores three nasty hits against the Captain. Fortunately for the Ultramarines champion, he wears an Iron Halo, a blessed device that bestows its bearer with a shield of protective energy against all but the most horrific of attacks. Andy has three crucial rolls to save the game. He succeeds on every roll, and shrugs off the Lord of Contagion's assault! Now it's Andy's turn to attack, and with the final dice roll of the game his Captain lashes out with a devastating riposte that cuts the Chaos lord apart. By slaying Nick's warlord and protecting the command bunker – even at great cost – the Ultramarines have won the day!

Whereas the Stormtalon initially dominated the battlefield, it simply cannot contend with the sheer number of attacks that Nick's Plague Drones can throw out.

Master-crafted steel rings on blighted, rusted iron as the two champions face off.

The Captain in Gravis armour emerges triumphant in a closely fought duel.

WANT TO PLAY
BIGGER BATTLES?

The Know No Fear starter set includes everything you need to fight big games.

- Two starter armies – the Death Guard and Primaris Space Marines. 31 miniatures!
- A guidebook containing in-depth background and rules.
- A full-colour game mat and scenery piece to battle across.
- Dice and a range ruler.

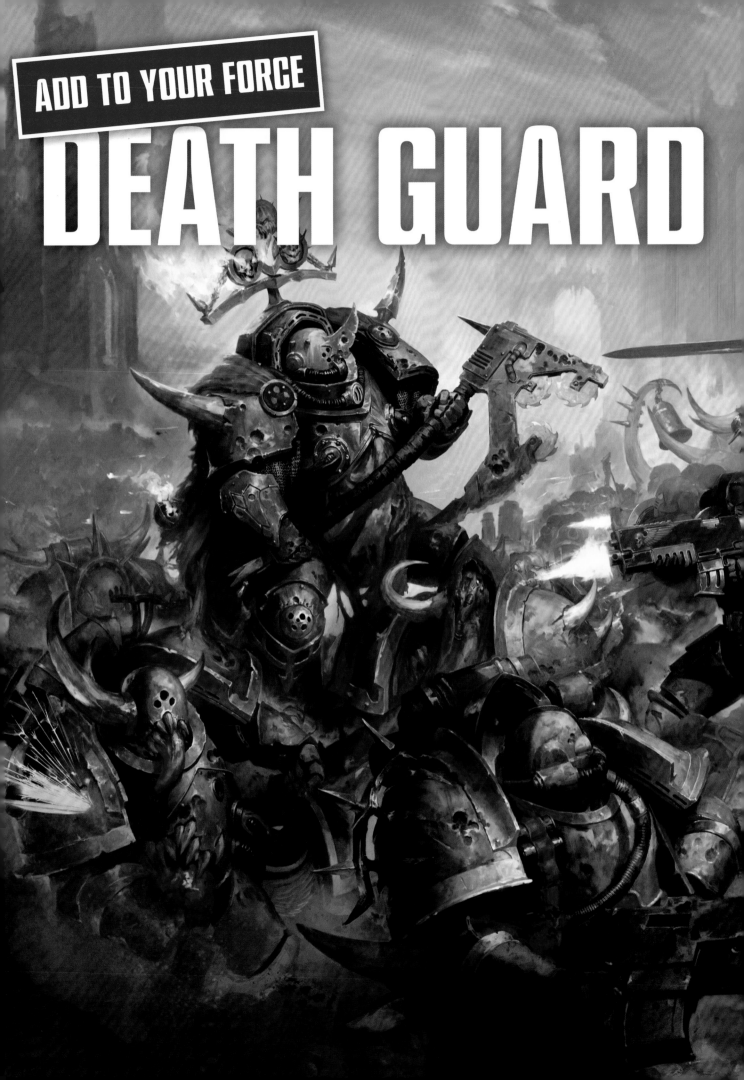

DEATH GUARD

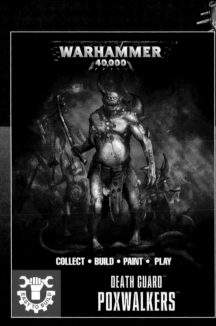

POX-RIDDEN CHAMPIONS OF CHAOS

WARHAMMER 40,000

COLLECT • BUILD • PAINT • PLAY

EASY TO BUILD

DEATH GUARD
PLAGUE MARINES

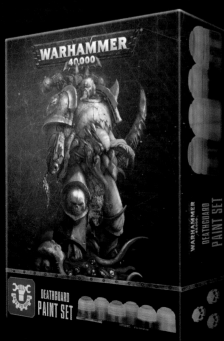

WARHAMMER 40,000

COLLECT • BUILD • PAINT • PLAY

EASY TO BUILD

DEATH GUARD
POXWALKERS

CORRUPTED PLAGUE SWARMS

WARHAMMER 40,000

DEATHGUARD
PAINT SET

Six paints: Agrax Earthshade, Armageddon Dust, Balthasar Gold, Death Guard Green, Leadbelcher and Rakarth Flesh, plus a Citadel Starter paint brush.

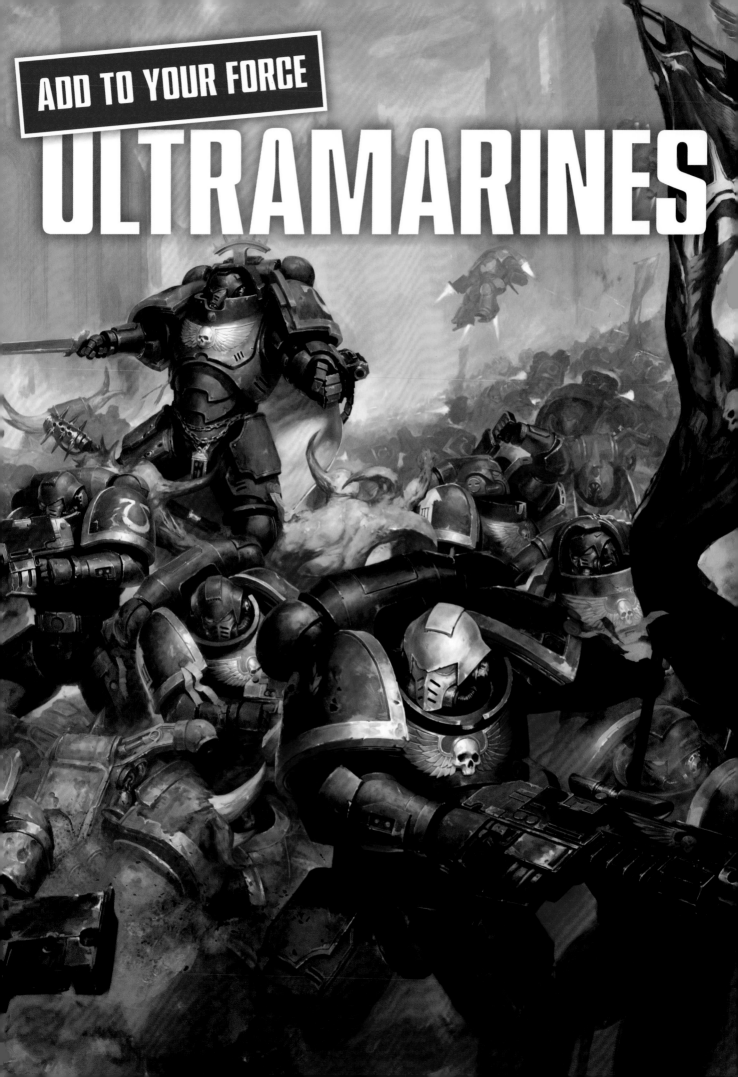

ADD TO YOUR FORCE
ULTRAMARINES

SUPERHUMAN ARMOURED WARRIORS

PRIMARIS SPACE MARINE INTERCESSORS

COLLECT • BUILD • PAINT • PLAY

DEADLY SHOCK TROOPS

PRIMARIS SPACE MARINE REIVERS

COLLECT • BUILD • PAINT • PLAY

Six paints: Agrax Earthshade, Armageddon Dust, Balthasar Gold, Bugman's Glow, Imperial Primer and Macragge Blue, plus a Citadel Starter paint brush.

SPACE WOLVES

14 Citadel Miniatures · WARHAMMER 40,000

The Space Wolves howl with battle-lust as they carve their way through their enemies in search of glory and renown.

ASTRA MILITARUM

13 Citadel Miniatures · WARHAMMER 40,000

The vast ranks of the Astra Militarum crush their enemies beneath countless booted feet.

BLOOD ANGELS

12 Citadel Miniatures · WARHAMMER 40,000

The Blood Angels descend into battle upon wings of smoke and flame.

MILITARUM TEMPESTUS

12 Citadel Miniatures · WARHAMMER 40,000

Disciplined to an almost inhuman degree, the Militarum Tempestus are an elite force that strikes with merciless precision.

TAU EMPIRE

23 Citadel Miniatures · WARHAMMER 40,000

Dynamic and determined, the Tau Empire is a rising star of conquest upon the galaxy's Eastern Fringe.

ELDAR

5 Citadel Miniatures · WARHAMMER 40,000

Tall, lithe and possessed of impossible grace, the Eldar are skilled beyond human imagining.

CHAOS SPACE MARINES

12 Citadel Miniatures · WARHAMMER 40,000

Warriors of the Dark Gods, the Chaos Space Marines wage an endless war against the Imperium of Man.

DARK ELDAR

15 Citadel Miniatures · WARHAMMER 40,000

The Dark Eldar are cruel corsairs who fight only for personal gain. They are possessed of technology so advanced it appears to be magic.

TYRANIDS

14 Citadel Miniatures · WARHAMMER 40,000

From beyond the gulf of intergalactic space come the Tyranids, an alien horror intent on consuming every living thing in their path.

ORKS

19 Citadel Miniatures · WARHAMMER 40,000

The air fills with bellowed war cries and the roar of smoke-belching engines as the Orks charge into battle.

NECRONS

17 Citadel Miniatures · WARHAMMER 40,000

Amidst the dark gulfs of space, the Necrons stir within their tomb worlds. Once, they ruled the stars like gods with their mighty armies and pitiless arrogance.

DEATHWATCH

12 Citadel Miniatures · WARHAMMER 40,000

The Deathwatch are the finest alien hunters in the Imperium, equipped with a profusion of wargear designed to slay tyrants and bring down monstrous horrors.

It is a time of heroes, and a time of monsters. A time of cataclysm and disaster, of impossible miracles and desperate, dwindling hope. Figures of legend bestride the Imperium once more, leading the forces of Humanity in the greatest conflict the galaxy will ever know. Yet on all fronts the warp-touched servants of the Chaos Gods close in, like hungry predators drawn to carrion. There is only war.

ETERNITY OF WAR

Across the galaxy, the Imperium is under attack on every front. Even so, some of these theatres of war have proven so costly, or are so so strategically vital, that their names resound through history.

WAR ZONE ULTRAMAR

Sweeping forth from the Scourge Stars come the Death Guard, favoured servants of the Plague God. Led by their forbidding Primach Mortarion, the Heretic Astartes launch a relentless assault across the Ultima Segmentum, spreading their sickening blight across hive cities and once-pristine agri worlds.

The realm of Ultramar, shining stellar empire of the Ultramarines, has long drawn the covetous eyes of the Ruinous Powers. Mortarion, lord of the Death Guard, has resolved to conquer and despoil the Ultramarines' realm in the name of the Plague God, Nurgle. Yet the Ultramarines are masterful strategists, courageous and noble warriors who strike back at the foul Death Guard on every front.

The Primarch Roboute Guilliman returns to his stricken domain alongside the forces of his galaxy-spanning Ultima Crusade, counter-attacking the forces of Chaos with cold fury and strategic brilliance. His Ultramarines rally and regroup, joined by their successor Chapters, Astra Militarum regiments and the forces of several Adeptus Mechanicus forge worlds.

Across Ultramar the Plague Wars escalate. The Greater Daemon of Nurgle Ku'Gath Plaguefather joins the fray, and on Parmenio his neverborn legions clash with Imperial Knights and the gargantuan war machines of the Collegia Titanica. On the ruined garden world of Iax, Guilliman himself takes to the field, facing the traitor Mortarion in single combat as a cataclysmic barrage of virus bombs chokes the skies with toxic clouds.

WAR ZONE CADIA

The fortress world of Cadia Prime – once the keystone of the Imperium's defence against the Chaos hordes of the Eye of Terror – was smashed into submission by Abaddon the Despoiler. Its ruined remains still lie at the heart of the Cadian Sector, a talismanic prize that the Imperium would dearly love to reclaim.

Ravaging warbands of Heretic Astartes maraud all throughout the Cadian Sector, with terrible new warlords rising daily from amongst their ranks. Many hurl themselves against the remaining Imperial worlds around Cadia Prime, extinguishing the lights of hope one at a time. Others war with one another, fighting over the spoils of shattered Imperial worlds, or competing to earn the blessings of the Dark Gods.

Daemonic legions spill through the sundered skin of reality from Thracian Primaris to Agripinaa, descending amidst howling warp storms to ravage the fortified worlds of the Cadian Sector. Every garrison, every Imperial warrior and warlord alike, must be ever watchful for the sudden onset of these most unnatural foes.

Fresh Imperial forces bolster the defences of War Zone Cadia despite the extreme hazards of this warp-ravaged region. Ships from the Great Exodus and scattered fragments of reinforcement fleets alike find their way to the fortified Imperial worlds, bringing fresh armies of the Astra Militarum, Adeptus Astartes, Adepta Sororitas and Adeptus Mechanicus into the fight.

WAR ZONE ARMAGEDDON

The smog-choked industrial world of Armageddon has been the site of several cataclysmic conflicts, and the horrific meat grinder that is the Third War for Armageddon has raged on for decades. Yet the planet's Astra Militarum defenders and its hordes of greenskin assailants are both utterly unprepared for the escalation to come.

Armageddon's Imperial regiments and their age-old Ork nemeses reel on the verge of obliteration. Summoned by centuries of bloodhsed, and empowered by the baleful emanations of the Great Rift, the Daemon Legions emerge and begin to use what remains of this broken world as an arena to settle ancient scores. The earth shakes as hosts led by Greater Daemons of all four Dark Gods clash in bouts of unimaginable carnage.

Baleful Warp energies seep out from the Great Rift, transforming the surface of Armageddon into a twisted hellscape. From countless wounds in reality pour baying Daemon legions, falling upon anything in their path in a frenzy of gore-splattered slaughter.

Madness and carnage rule across Armageddon. The planet's grim industrial jungle is warped by the power of Chaos, creating a nightmarish, trap-strewn wilderness littered with flesh-factories, crematoria and geysers of flesh-melting acid. The three factions battle across this roiling insanity in an apocalyptic ground war, the like of which even battle-weary Armageddon has never seen before.

CITADEL MINIATURES SHOWCASE

The showcase on the following pages demonstrates the epic grandeur of just a sample of the Warhammer 40,000 miniatures range. These inspiring examples have all been painted by Games Workshop's 'Eavy Metal team – amongst the greatest professional miniature painters in the world. From towering monsters to mighty heroes, the 'Eavy Metal painters render Games Workshop's vast range of Citadel Miniatures in jaw-dropping detail for all to marvel at.

Ultramarines Captain in Gravis Armour

Ultramarines Inceptor Sergeant

Ultramarines Ancient

Imperial Fists Tactical Marine

Ultramarines Devastator Marine

Ultramarines Assault Marine

Blood Angels Furioso Dreadnought

Blood Angels Intercessor

Dark Angels Intercessor

The Yncarne, Avatar of Ynnead

Harlequin Shadowseer

Yvraine, Emissary of Ynnead

Drukhari Wracks

Craftworlds Wraithguard

Craftworlds Farseer

Craftworlds Wraithknight

Adeptus Mechanicus Tech-Priest Dominus

Adeptus Mechanicus Kastelan Robot

Adeptus Mechanicus Skitarii Vanguard

Black Legion Raptor

Crimson Slaughter Helbrute

Death Guard Noxious Blightbringer

Death Guard Plague Marine

Chaos Daemons Bloodthirster of Unfettered Fury

Ork Warboss

Ork Flash Git

Tyranids Tyrant Guard

Genestealer Cults Patriarch

Genestealer Cults Hybrid Metamorph

Genestealer Cults Neophyte Hybrid

T'au Empire XV8 Crisis Battlesuit

T'au Empire XV95 Ghostkeel Battlesuit

PAINTING MINIATURES

The dark future of Warhammer 40,000 offers infinite possibilities for any avid miniature collector. Its vast armies and apocalyptic battles are fuel for your own creative journey, inspiring you to build and paint your amazing collection.

'There's no right or wrong way to go about this – you should go wherever your inspiration takes you, and do whatever you think makes your miniatures look great.'

One of the greatest joys of collecting Citadel Miniatures can be found in the modelling and painting of your collection, as you assemble and recreate the great champions, terrifying war engines and strange alien landscapes of the Imperium and beyond. Nothing beats seeing a fully painted army deployed upon a carefully crafted tabletop battlefield complete with towering fortifications and fantastical scenery, or else set up in a display case to be admired by all.

There's real satisfaction to be had in putting your own mark upon your miniatures, bringing them to life with a paintbrush and teasing out all of the finely sculpted detail of each model. Some people revel in treating each individual miniature as its own work of art, lavishing attention on every inch and building scenic bases. Others prefer to assemble vast legions of warriors in matching liveries, focussing on the spectacle of massed ranks, armed and ready for war.

There's no right or wrong way to go about this – you should go wherever your inspiration takes you, and do whatever you think makes your miniatures look great.

Take your time to consider; the paint scheme you select will help you to imbue your models with character and story, and to define who they are. Why has this particular strike force of Space Marines got pockmarked, battle-scarred armour? Why do they bear a silver sword campaign badge upon their left knee-pads? Why are they defending this towering string of defensive bastions amidst the smouldering hell of a volcanic death world? With an ever-growing range of evocative Citadel Miniatures to choose from, the choice is yours – what exciting story do you want to tell with your miniatures?

A PERSONAL TOUCH

Before painting your models, you'll first need to assemble them. To begin with, you'll want to follow the advice given in the construction booklet supplied with your models. As your confidence grows, you may find yourself trying more ambitious methods, leading to more personalised results and modelling conversions.

Many factions, including the Adeptus Astartes and Heretic Astartes both, use proud or infernal heraldry to unite them better upon the battlefield. You might want to paint your collection to match those we have created for Warhammer 40,000. You may be inspired by a photo or piece of artwork, or choose to replicate a particular faction's look. Alternatively, you might wish to create a brand new colour scheme of your own devising, along with the icons to go with it. After all, this is your army, your story and your hobby – the direction you take is up to you!

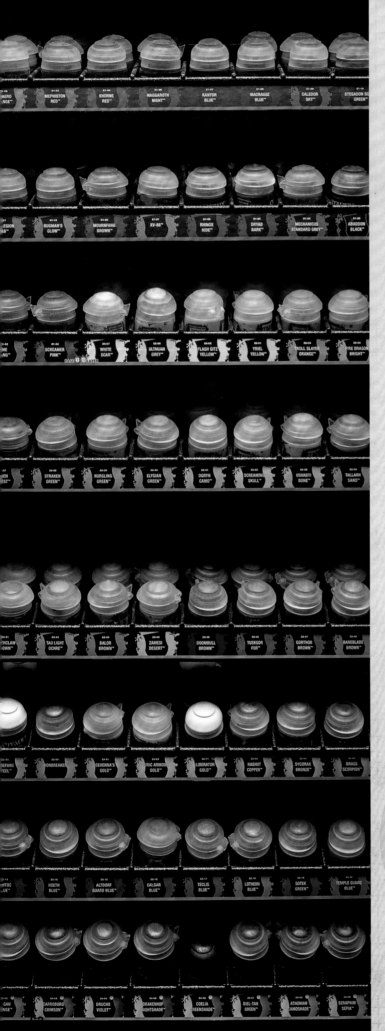

THE CITADEL PAINT SYSTEM

Painting Citadel Miniatures is one of the most creative and enjoyable aspects of the Warhammer 40,000 hobby, and is an essential element of making the most of your miniatures collection. In this feature, we examine the Citadel Paint System, and show you how you can use it to achieve fantastic results.

One thing that unites almost every collector of Citadel Miniatures is the desire to own beautifully painted armies of our favourite models, whether to conquer all before them on the tabletop battlefield or simply to admire and display.

To help with this universal goal, Games Workshop has created the Citadel Paint System. This revolutionary combination of techniques, tools and paints makes painting straightforward, easy to learn and most importantly fun! Using the Citadel Paint System, you choose the colours you want to paint your models, select the techniques you want to use on them, and apply these in a few simple steps for what will be some great results. These pages take you through it, step by step, technique by technique.

To explain it all, we've included advice from our army painters and the 'Eavy Metal team. The army painters are masters of creating the vast armies and comprehensive painting guides that you will see in our various publications, while the 'Eavy Metal team use years of hard-earned skills to produce individual masterpieces that showcase our Citadel Miniatures. Read on…

COLOUR COMBINATIONS

Games Workshop produce a range of painting guides for different armies and colour schemes, which are a great way to learn which paints to use to achieve a particular colour or effect. The Warhammer TV YouTube channel is also a fantastic source of inspiration and advice – check it out.

WARHAMMER TV

PAINTING TECHNIQUES

TECHNIQUE 1: BASECOATING (PG 66)

The foundation upon which the entire paint system is based, a well-applied basecoat gives your model a smooth starting point for later stages. Basecoats use Citadel Base paints, with their high pigment content and excellent coverage.

TECHNIQUE 2: SHADING (PG 67)

Shading is a technique that brings out all of the subtle details and textures on your model using Citadel Shades. Formulated to flow into recesses, Shades provide natural, effective shading to define the details on your miniatures.

TECHNIQUE 3: DRYBRUSHING (PG 68)

Drybrushing is an excellent technique for capturing raised details and creating natural highlights on models, especially those with a lot of small details or sharp edges. Citadel Dry paints are designed to make this much-loved method of painting as straightforward as possible.

TECHNIQUE 4: LAYERING (PG 69)

Layering is the method by which painters use increasingly lighter colours to create highlights on the raised areas of models by adding layers of lighter colour. Citadel Layer paints are formulated with a certain translucency so they can be applied over Base paints and each other with great results.

5 GLAZING (PG 70)

Glazing is an advanced technique that many experienced painters use to great effect on their miniatures, primarily to intensify an area of colour. Citadel Glazes are special paints that can make the basecoats and layers on your models really stand out, or unify areas on your models where the colours might be a little too bright or the layering too stark.

Citadel Glazes are also designed to sit on the miniature where they are applied, unlike Citadel Shades, which will naturally flow into the recesses on a model and add shading and definition to them.

6 BASING (PG 71)

A miniature is never truly finished until it has been based. Citadel Texture paint is the perfect way to ensure all the bases in your army have brilliant, consistent finishes.

Citadel Texture paint can be applied directly onto the bases of your painted models, and it dries quickly leaving an effective, contoured finish. You can either leave this just as it is, or shade and paint it like any other part of the model. You can even add grass tufts for a finishing touch.

7 TECHNICAL PAINTS (PG 72)

Technical paints are designed to help you achieve a range of effects, from creating rust and corrosion to the foetid slurry of Nurgle's Rot or the gore of Blood for the Blood God. The range also includes Agrellan Earth and Martian Ironearth for creating dry, cracked ground, and the Citadel Gem paints collection for achieving stunning effects on gems and jewels.

BRUSHES

The Citadel range of brushes has been designed from the ground up by our Studio painters, specifically for use with the Citadel Paint System. Each brush works best for a particular technique, so you can get the best results on all your models.

BASE

Base brushes have tough-wearing bristles designed to survive the rigours of basecoating your models. There are four sizes (S, M, L and XL) so that you can tackle any painting challenge. You'll notice that larger brushes have a broad, flat head, which is perfect for ensuring your basecoat covers your models, and the thinner, chisel-like ends are ideal for painting neatly up to the edges of areas.

DRY

Drybrushing is an unusual technique, in that it can be quite hard on your brushes, so the Dry range are made to be especially rugged and durable.

CHOOSE YOUR WEAPONS!

Taken as a whole, the wide range of Citadel brushes available could seem daunting to a beginner, but fear not! Just like collecting an army or building up your palette of paints, you can start with the basics and work up from there.

Once you move beyond the Citadel starter brush, the best place to go next is to pick up a small layer brush, and a medium base brush. With these two finely crafted painting implements at your disposal, you will have a great start to your brush collection, and be able to attempt all of the techniques detailed on the following pages with confidence.

Of course, there's nothing like using the right tool for the right job, and as your confidence and skill grows you will want to look into all the other sorts of Citadel brushes. As a good foundation to build upon, however, these two brushes are the choice of the professionals!

CARE TIPS

1. Wash your brush regularly. Keep a pot of clean, cold water on standby to wash your brush out with. Swirl the brush vigorously in the water to clean it – but don't grind the bristles against the edge or bottom. You should wash your brush often – any time you notice a change in the flow of paint as you are working and when you change colours.

2. Never let paint reach the ferrule (that metal area of the brush just past the bristles is the ferrule). Never dip your brush so far into the paint that it touches this, or when it dries, your bristles will splay out. If you get some paint in there by accident, wash the brush thoroughly.

3. Always use the largest brush suitable for the job. You will be surprised how, with a little practice, you can use a much larger brush than you expected to get the same result. Using a larger brush speeds up the process nicely, and helps ensure smooth results.

4. Keep a sharp point. Maintain the point on your brush by twisting the bristles softly against your palette. Check out our how to paint videos online for examples.

LAYER

Layer brushes are perfect for applying layer paints. This tends to be precise work, and they have fine heads and soft bristles accordingly.

SHADE

There are two Citadel Shade brushes, the M and the L. Both have bristles designed to hold the maximum amount of Shade as you draw it over your models. For most tasks you'll want to use the M Shade brush as the sharp point allows you to apply Shades with accuracy. The L Brush is for particularly large models.

GLAZE

Glazing tends to be quite precise, so the Glaze brush has synthetic bristles to keep its point while you work.

TEXTURE

The M Texture tool is a spreader for applying Texture paints to your models and their bases. Use the large end to scoop the paint from the pot, and the narrow end to spread it across the surface.

SCENERY

The Citadel Scenery brushes are extra large brushes with coarse bristles – ideal for quickly getting a lot of coverage on the large spaces of boards and scenery.

UNDERCOATING

Undercoating helps paint adhere to your models and also helps prevent it from flaking off. Most people use an undercoat spray, enabling them to undercoat whole units quickly and neatly.

There are a number of spray-paints in the Citadel range, from Chaos Black and Corax White to Leadbelcher and Macragge Blue. If you're new to using spray paint, make sure you read the instructions on the can carefully before you start. When undercoating models, do it outside in a well-ventilated area and well away from things you value (such as your car or pets). We recommend using a spray stick (see bottom-right) to hold your models, so you can spray the models from every angle without having to touch them while they are still wet.

Before spraying, shake the spray can for at least two minutes to that the paint and propellant mix properly. Less shaking than this, and you could end up with streaky paint, a cloudy finish or, worse, a totally ruined model. It's worth reiterating: two minutes, no less! Always keep the spray can upright, too, otherwise the spray mix may come out inconsistently.

When spraying your models, a quick burst from the spray can (less than a second) from around 8-12 inches is more effective than a prolonged barrage at closer range, which can obscure the details of your models and leave them dripping with paint. Work around the model, undercoating it in short, quick blasts until the whole miniature is evenly undercoated. Again, a spray stick is handy for this as it helps economise on how much paint you use and enables you to turn the models around without having to handle them, which would risk smudging the undercoat.

Lastly, when you're done undercoating your models, clean out the nozzle of the spray can by turning it upside down and spraying until only gas comes out. This prevents the nozzle from clogging, ruining the can.

OPTIMAL CONDITIONS

Avoid spraying if it is too hot or cold outside. When it's too cold, the paint struggles to dry, leaving it streaky; too hot and the paint particles dry before they reach your model, making the paint grainy. Between 15 and 25 degrees centigrade is ideal.

FOR A RAINY DAY...

Sometimes, such as when it's cold outside, you may want to undercoat a model by hand. For this you'll need a pot of Imperial Primer and the largest Base brush you can use for the task. Simply apply the Primer like you would a basecoat.

The Intercessor on the left was undercoated with Macragge Blue spray, while the model on the right was undercoated with Chaos Black spray. A coloured undercoat is great for models that will display large areas of that colour – this would be a great way to start painting your Primaris Space Marines as Ultramarines or Crimson Fists, for example. A black undercoat is ideal for darker miniatures, and provides deeper shading.

For our spray sticks we use a piece of wood about two feet long. Stick a strip of double-sided tape along the top and gently attach your models to it, leaving a little space between them. Secured in this way, the spray stick can be held at any angle so you can spray every part of the models. We recommend wearing a latex glove on the hand holding the stick to avoid accidentally undercoating your fingers.

BASECOATING

A basecoat provides the first layer of paint you apply to a model after the undercoat and forms the foundation of every other colour on the model – indeed, the foundation of the entire paint job itself – so read on for the essentials and a few top tips from the masters.

Basecoating is the first painting technique you'll apply to your miniatures and, if done well, will make painting your models much easier and more enjoyable. Many painting frustrations can be alleviated with a neat, smooth basecoat right from the start.

There are four Base brushes in the Citadel brush range. Always use the largest one you can for the job. Not only does it make painting easier, it also makes it much faster. The Intercessor shown below was painted using an L Base brush and took only a couple of minutes to basecoat.

While there is a temptation to use the paint straight out of the pot, always water it down. Firstly, this stops you applying the paint too thickly. Two thin coats of paint are better than one thick one – a mantra that is well worth keeping in mind whenever painting your miniatures! Remember, you can

always put more paint on a model but you can't take it off. Secondly, a dab of water stops the paint from drying out on the palette, which can make it go thick and tacky, leading to a lumpy, uneven basecoat.

1 When getting paint out of the pot, use your brush to take a small amount from the lid rather than dunking the brush into the pot itself.

2 Put the paint on a palette and mix in about half as much water as there is paint. Pulling the brush towards you, coat the bristles in paint.

3 As mentioned in the brushes section, never get paint on the ferrule. An even application halfway up the bristles is easily enough paint.

4 Using the flat of the brush, the basecoat (in this case Macragge Blue) is applied to the model in smooth, even coats, focussing on the larger armour plates.

5 The thin edge, rather than the wide flat side of the brush, can then be used for smaller areas of the model such as the hands.

6 Once the basecoat is dry, check it for any streaky areas and re-apply the colour to get a smooth, even finish where necessary.

SHADING

Shading your models with Citadel Shades creates areas of rich, darker colour that accentuate the natural shadows on the miniature – perfect for capturing all that detail and creating a sense of depth across the model.

Citadel Shades are much thinner than other paints, specially formulated to flow into the recesses and around the details on your miniatures. The perfect follow-up to a good basecoat, shading provides your miniatures with effortless, natural depth.

Typically, you will apply a Shade before you begin layering or drybrushing your model – it settles into the recesses and around the details, making those areas look more pronounced. Sometimes,

you might use a Shade later on in the painting process, which can be useful for staining the layers of paint below. Either way, there are three main shading techniques; all-over shades, section shades and recess shades. The first two cover large areas of the model, either all of it or particular sections, while a recess shade focusses on neatly applying the Shade to specific recesses.

Citadel Shade brushes have bristles designed to hold plenty of liquid, so you

can apply the Shade simply by painting it on; as you press your brush against the model, the Shade will flow out, and you can use your brush to move the Shade around to where you need it.

Because Shades are much thinner than other paints, they will take a bit longer to dry. Factor this in when you are painting – once you've applied your Shades, set the model on the side for half an hour or so. While one model dries, you can be painting another.

Before you use any Citadel Shade, make sure the lid is firmly closed and shake it vigorously to ensure the flow of medium is well mixed in.

Use your M Shade brush to take paint from the pot and transfer it to your palette. Citadel Shades do not need to be watered down.

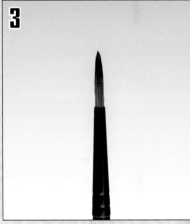

When you apply Citadel Shades, your brush should not be overloaded – aim for a saturation like you can see in this example.

Apply the Shade to your model in a painting motion, using the brush to ensure it flows into all of the recesses and over the details.

Sometimes you only want to shade the recesses of a model. In these cases, use a smaller brush so you can paint more precisely.

Once you have applied the Shade, give it plenty of time to dry. As it dries, it leaves rich colours within all the crevices, adding depth.

DRYBRUSHING

Drybrushing is a fantastic technique for quickly capturing all the raised details on a model and providing subtle and effective highlights. Here, we show you the essentials and how the Studio army painters use drybrushing to take their own paint jobs to the next level.

Drybrushing is a technique beloved by painters everywhere, useful for everything from highlighting the metallic bodies of Necron Warriors to painting the hulls of battle tanks and combat aircraft. Essentially, the technique consists of rapidly brushing your Dry brush against the detailed areas of a model to capture all the raised details with a light dusting of paint.

Drybrushing is very simple, as you can see in the stages below. Basically, having loaded your brush with Dry paint, you proceed to wipe most of it off on a piece of tissue or paper towel. This leaves you with a small amount of very 'dry' paint on the bristles – a little paint goes a long way. As you brush the bristles against the models, you'll see the paint transfer. The longer you brush, the heavier the coverage will be. When it seems like you are running low on paint on your bristles, you simply reload your brush with more paint, wipe off the excess as before and start again.

The beauty of drybrushing is that the results are instant. You can gauge the effect as you go along and decide if the coverage is sufficient and the highlight light enough, or whether you want to continue drybrushing. Because of this, drybrushing is often the stage where you can most clearly see your paint job coming to fruition as highlights appear on the edges, contrasting with the areas of deep colour left by your earlier shading, and the model nears completion.

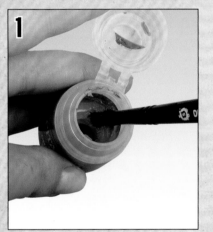

First, load some Dry paint onto your brush directly from the pot. There's no need to take too much paint – just use a little bit at a time.

Wipe off the excess paint from your brush onto a piece of tissue or paper towel. You should remove almost all of the paint, as shown here.

With the paint removed, your brush should look like this. You can see a little paint remaining on the bristles – this is enough for drybrushing.

Next, gently brush the bristles against your model in a quick back-and-forth motion to transfer the paint to the raised areas.

For models with large, flat areas like Space Marines, don't drybrush the whole surface. Try to focus on the edges and stay out of the recesses.

By using lighter and lighter colours, you can do incremental highlights with Dry paints, like Hoeth Blue after Macragge Blue for the Ultramarines.

LAYERING

Layering is a painting technique designed to bring life and realism to your miniatures by accentuating the raised areas of a model. Done well, the end result is a beautifully painted model with natural-looking highlights that really stands out on the battlefield.

There are two main techniques to layer: the solid layer and the highlight. A solid layer, as shown in image 3, is designed to cover a whole section of a model while leaving the basecoat and the shade visible in the recesses.

This has the dramatic effect of changing the colour of a model. Because Layer paints have a thinner consistency than Base paints, applying a Layer in this way may require several coats of paint to cover darker colours beneath.

Just like basecoating, a few thin layers are better than one thick layer – take your time, apply your layers neatly, and you'll get a smooth, even finish.

Highlighting is another form of layering, designed to simulate the effect of light catching the raised edges of your miniatures. Light naturally catches the most prominent edges of an object, be it the keen edge of a Space Marine power sword or the ridged plates of a Tyranid's chitinous armour. This is why

highlights are only applied sparingly to a miniature and normally only to raised areas as shown in images 4 to 6. A final highlight to a sword or face is often the last technique to be applied to a miniature, the finishing touch to all your hard work and a moment to be relished.

1 Gently rotate the brush when drawing paint from your palette. This will help you keep the tip of the brush as fine and pointy as possible.

2 Ensure there's not too much paint on your Layer brush. It should be evenly distributed on the bristles, and never cover so much as to reach the ferrule.

3 When layering across large areas, always try to keep the brush strokes going in the same direction to minimise streaks, lines and patchy sections.

4 Apply any highlights to the very edges of each area. Be sure to wash your brush regularly so as to prevent any paint from drying in the bristles.

5 For highlights along the edge of a detail (such as an armour panel), use the edge of the brush, as it will give you a better control than the tip.

6 Apply a final highlight, but only to the most prominent edges of the model. This simulates light falling naturally on the model from above.

GLAZING

Glazing is a handy technique that can be used to intensify the colours on a miniature. Though similar in appearance to Citadel Shades, Glazes work in a very different way and with a different purpose. Read on to find out how they will enhance your painting.

Glazes are translucent inks that are designed to alter the hue of a colour, making it stronger and more vibrant. They are perfect for drawing attention to parts of a model that you want to capture the viewer's attention – flames, energised blades, faces, glowing energy sources and so on.

They are also especially handy when you get towards finishing a model and find that your highlights have de-saturated a colour. This often happens

with bright colours such as red and yellow. Depending on your highlight colours, red can take on a pastel hue that borders on yellow or pink, while yellow can end up looking like cream or bone. A Glaze over the whole area will bring back the vibrancy of the original colour (the basecoat or layer beneath) and gently tone down excessive highlighting, resulting in a much smoother transition between the colours, as can be seen in the images below.

Glazes are also great on their own and can even be applied directly over a Corax White undercoat with dramatic effect, as shown on this Intercessor's helmet-lenses.

When glazing large areas, the M Shade brush is usually the best tool for the job, as it can hold a lot of paint in its bristles and still offer good precision.

A Glaze should be applied more like a Layer than a Shade – in broad, fluid strokes that cover the whole area without pooling in the recesses.

Glazes stain the colours beneath them while not obscuring them. The original colour shows through because of the Glaze's translucent quality.

GEMSTONE PAINTS

Painting gemstones and reflective surfaces is often one of the trickiest tasks for a hobbyist. With the aid of the Gemstone paints in Citadel's Technical range, however, it couldn't be easier to get that vibrant sparkle from crystal and glass surfaces.

To begin with, simply base the desired area with a metallic paint – Stormhost Silver is a great choice, but you can also experiment with colours like Liberator Gold or Skullcrusher Brass for a unique effect. Then apply the Technical paint over the top. There is lots of room for experimentation with this simple technique. It's a great way to paint tricky details like Space Marine helmet lenses or rifle scopes, for example.

BASING

A Citadel Miniature isn't completely finished until its base has been transformed from flat plastic into an evocative battlescape. This maxim is as true for the rank and file infantry in your army as it is for the most glorious and eye-catching centrepiece model.

With your model fully painted, all that remains is to complete it with a great-looking base. Citadel Texture paints are designed with a mixture of coarse and fine grit set into the paint mix so that you can paint them straight onto the bases of your models and they will dry leaving an awesome textured finish.

At its most simple, you can just apply a layer of Citadel Texture paint to your base and, once it is dry, you'll have a good result. The best finishes, however, come when you take a little time to add a few extra details.

A Citadel Shade applied over the Texture paint will pick out all the nuances of the grit, and a drybrush over the top creates a brilliant sense of depth and detail that will really complete your model.

With Texture paints, bear in mind that the thicker, grainier composition of the paint can damage your brushes (which will also struggle to move the Texture paint around the base) – use an M Texture spreader to apply them instead. Also, always make sure you give them plenty of time to dry before adding any more paint.

1 Use the broad head of your M Texture tool to scoop out a glob of texture paint. Take a little at a time to help you place it neatly on your base.

2 Spread the Texture paint around the surface of the base. Use the narrow head of the Texture tool to carefully spread it around, covering the entire base.

3 Once the Texture paint has fully dried (this can take around 45 minutes depending on the thickness), apply a Shade to emphasise all the textures.

4 Finally, once the Shade is dry, give the top of the base a drybrush to complete the look, and apply a basecoat around the base's rim to tidy it up.

DETAIL BASES

A textured base is great, but it looks so much better with some extra details such as grass tufts or some spare skulls. Alternatively, if you really want to make your models stand out, why not pick up a pack of the Sector Imperialis bases – each one a detailed piece in its own right that boasts grilles, flagstones, skulls and the like – and base your models with these?

TECHNICAL PAINTS

Blood, pus, rust, and sun-parched earth; these are the hallmarks of the Technical paints, a range of special effects paints that allow you to bring the horrors of war to life on your miniatures. From leaking slime to spatterings of fresh gore, these paints make such effects easy and fun to achieve.

Technical paints are usually some of the last paint you'll use on your miniatures, as they provide the finishing touches to your paint job. They are made to add that extra level of realism to a miniature and, as such, are each designed with a specific effect in mind, such as glossy bile or freshly spilt blood, though with a little imagination you can find plenty more uses for them over time.

Despite their name, Technical paints are not hard to use, especially if you follow these tips from the Studio army painters. Indeed, splattering Blood for the Blood God all over a miniature can be quite satisfying! You can find out more about Technical paints on our YouTube channel, Warhammer TV, which features videos of this technique in action, so you can see how it's done.

LAHMIAN MEDIUM

Lahmian Medium has two uses, though both are very different. Lahmian Medium is actually paint without a pigment and, as such, it is perfect for reducing the opacity of a coloured paint without affecting its chemical make-up (unlike water, which would dilute it). This is very handy for blending colours on a model or creating your own glazes. Lahmian Medium can also be used as a matt varnish, which is ideal for sealing transfers securely to your miniatures. Simply apply it as you would a Glaze with the M Glaze brush.

NIHILAKH OXIDE

Nihilakh Oxide is perfect for creating a corroded copper, bronze or brass effect. It has a thin consistency that is best applied with the M Glaze brush – a little bit will give you a light effect, while a loaded brush (1) will give you a much deeper, milkier finish like real-life verdigris. Here we have painted Nihilakh Oxide around the bronze details on a Foetid Bloat-drone (2), making them look ancient and corroded.

Top Tip: Paint Nihilakh Oxide straight over a Corax White undercoat for ethereal energies and baleful flames.

TYPHUS CORROSION AND RYZA RUST

These paints work together to create realistic rust effects on your miniatures. Typhus Corrosion is like a thick Shade that contains particles of grit which add texture to a model. Apply liberally with the M Shade brush (1) over the area you want to look rusty then let it dry. Then, using the S Drybrush, gently drybrush a layer of Ryza Rust over it (2) to make it look like filthy, peeling rust.

Top Tip: Paint Ironbreaker around the edges of the metal to show where the rust has scraped off.

BLOOD FOR THE BLOOD GOD

Khorne's favourite paint, Blood for the Blood God is specifically designed to look like sticky, glistening and, most importantly, freshly spilled blood. Applying it is easy. Use an S Layer brush to drag the paint across the blades and armour of your models (1). You can even apply some to an S Dry brush and pull your finger across the bristles to 'flick' it onto your models, creating a spatter effect (2). The more you do, the gorier the model will be!

Top Tip: Less is more. Start with a little and build it up to create a realistic effect.

MARTIAN IRONEARTH AND AGRELLAN EARTH

These two are cracking paints. They actually crack as they dry, creating realistic-looking, sun-parched ground for your models to fight over. Load up the M Base brush with a large glob of this thick paint and apply it to your model's base, being careful of their feet (1). Leave the model somewhere warm overnight to let the paint crack (2).

Top Tip: Paint a layer of PVA glue onto the model's base first, let it dry, then apply the cracking paint. The cracks will be even bigger!

NURGLE'S ROT

The Plague Lord's most fecund blessing in paint form, Nurgle's Rot sets as a glistening residue. We recommend using an M Glaze brush for precision, loaded with a generous glob of Nurgle's Rot (1). Paint it on as you would a Citadel Shade – just be aware that it's a little more viscous, so you'll need to poke it around a little with your bristles to get it in the recesses (2).

Top Tip: The thicker you paint it on, the more opaque Nurgle's Rot is, so build it up in layers to get your desired liquid effect.

'ARDCOAT

'Ardcoat is a gloss varnish that has multiple uses. When applying transfers, apply a layer of 'Ardcoat to the area first to help smooth over any bumps or ridges created during the painting process – it will make the transfer adhere much more easily. 'Ardcoat also works brilliantly as an effect paint. Applied over sorcerous flames, magic swords and gemstones, it gives them a shiny, magical quality. Lastly, 'Ardcoat can, of course, be used as a gloss varnish to protect your miniatures from the rigours of battle.

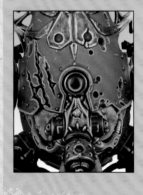

CITADEL AIR PAINTS

Another advanced technique that some people use is to apply their paints using a device known as an airbrush. By atomising the paint and spraying it onto the model in incredibly thin layers, this tool allows painters to achieve smooth blending and colour transitions that are virtually impossible to achieve by hand. For those who use airbrushes, Games Workshop produces a range of Citadel paints in airbrush format, along with a carefully formulated cleaning fluid to prevent clogging.

INTERCESSOR

In this section we show how to bring your heroic Space Marines to life using the paints in the Ultramarines Paint Set. This straightforward guide features an Intercessor Marine, but the same basic techniques can be used for any of your Ultramarines models.

Intercessor Squads form the core of a Primaris Space Marine strike force. Armed with accurate and devastating bolt rifles, they are capable of unleashing a truly ferocious storm of fire, pinning their foes down with the precision and rapidity of their assault before blasting them to pieces. Each Intercessor battle-brother also carries a complement of frag and krak grenades, enabling them to engage and destroy both infantry and light vehicles. While these warriors are peerless ranged combatants able to outgun almost any foe, they are also at home in the blood and thunder of melee combat. Blessed by the most advanced genetic science in the Imperium, Intercessor Marines can snap an Ork's neck with a twist of their gauntlets, stand strong in the face of the most hideous warp-spawned monstrosities, and endure even the the most appalling battlefield conditions. As the Imperium slips ever closer to oblivion, such redoubtable courage and martial skill will be in ever greater need.

1 To begin, use Macragge Blue to paint an undercoat all over the model, ensuring that you get a nice, even coverage.

2 Next, basecoat your model. Apply Balthasar Gold to the trim of the shoulder pads and the aquila on the chestplate, Imperial Primer to the bolter and Bugman's Glow to any parchment.

3 Next, apply Agrax Earthshade all over the model to define the recesses of the Intercessor's armour and weapons.

4 To complete your Intercessor Marine, apply a thick coat of Armageddon Dust to the base. You can also paint the rim of the base with Imperial Primer to help the model stand out.

REIVER

Unlike the front-line Intercessor Squads, some of the Primaris Reivers eschew the iconic Space Marine helmet in favour of an intimidating half-mask. The process below includes painting this sergeant's hair and skin, and can be applied to any similar models in your collection.

1

Begin with an undercoat of Macragge Blue all over the model. Make sure that you end up with an even coverage over the whole miniature.

2

Next, apply the basecoats. First, carefully apply Bugman's Glow to the skin. Use Balthasar Gold for the shoulder pad trim and knife detail, and Imperial Primer for the model's hair, weapons and pouches.

3

Follow up with a shade of Agrax Earthshade to define the recesses of the Reiver's Mk X Phobos armour and bring out his facial detail – apply this all over the model.

4

To finish your Reiver, add a thick coat of Armageddon Dust to the surface he's standing on. Painting the rim of the base with Imperial Primer is a great final touch.

All Space Marines are experts of the rapid strike, but Reiver Squads take such skills to the next level. They are specially trained and equipped to launch brutally effective and unexpected assaults. They do so with a sudden fury and shocking violence, for the Reiver Squads are intended as terror troops to sow fear and confusion amongst their foes. There is nothing that can prepare an enemy for the savage suddenness with which a Reiver attack comes. Emerging from some unforeseen angle, the Reiver Squad launch themselves into battle amidst the raucous noise and explosions of shock grenades. The time for silence is over, replaced with a cacophony of sounds that barrage the auditory senses – wave-amplified blasts of specially modified bolt carbines, the keening of slicing combat blades, and the augmented guttural roars of the warriors themselves. Moving quickly, shooting and slashing at superhuman speeds, the Reiver Squad annihilate their targets. Such an unpredictable assault is enough to set off a chain reaction of panic that ripples down the enemy line as the roaring Reivers move to bring down their next target.

PLAGUE MARINE

As favoured children of Nurgle, the Death Guard are blessed with multitudinous gifts, from horn-like growths to weeping buboes. Using the paints in the Death Guard Paint Set, you can ensure your Plague Marine models display the foetid glory of the Lord of Decay.

Plague Marines advance out of the smoke and fog of the battlefield, marching on implacably even as enemy fire spatters off their filth-encrusted armour, and unleashing a battering torrent of bolter fire in return. Hulking figures whose rotting flesh has fused with the ancient suits of power armour that they wear, Plague Marines are immune to pain and fatigue, and horrendously difficult to kill. Their patron Nurgle, God of Decay, has blessed them with manifold gifts, including layers of thick, rancid fat which soak up lasfire, blasts and bolts, as well as thick, bony protrusions that can deflect even a well-aimed sword thrust. The Plague Marines' bolters are caked with decayed matter, and they wield jagged plague knives which bubble and seethe with foul toxins. When they near their foe, they will hurl their blight grenades into the thick of the enemy ranks, to burst in a cloud of pathogenic spores and caustic slime. As the Plague Marines march, clouds of flies swirl around them in a droning choir, masking the gurgling chuckles of the Heretic Astartes as they bring the bountiful treasures of Nurgle to their victims.

First of all, paint the Plague Marine with an undercoat of Death Guard Green. Make sure you get a nice, even covering across the model.

Next, apply your basecoats. Use Leadbelcher for the bolter and Balthasar Gold for the armour trim and raised areas on the model's wargear. Finish with Rakarth Flesh for bones and skin.

An all-over shade of Agrax Earthshade will give depth to the Plague Marine's armour, and give him the perfect grimy, unwashed look.

Finally, finish the model off by applying a thick coat of Armageddon Dust to its base. After the texture paint dries, you can shade or drybrush it as you see fit, or simply leave it as it is.

POXWALKER

Unfortunate victims of the Death Guard's potent strains of disease, Poxwalkers are riddled with foul lesions and mutations. A simple combination of painting techniques can really capture the putrid corruption of these shambling horrors.

1

Just as we did with the Plague Marine, start off by painting your Poxwalker with a thorough undercoat of Death Guard Green.

2

Basecoat the Poxwalker's pallid skin with Rakarth Flesh, its weapon with Leadbelcher, and any symbols or other items with Balthasar Gold.

3

Next, apply an all-over shade of Agrax Earthshade, making sure that you cover every recess and detail on the model.

4

All that's left to do is to apply a thick coat of Armageddon Dust to your festering Poxwalker's base.

Shambling, pox-ridden horrors swathed in buboes and lesions, Poxwalkers are victims of the foul affliction known as the Walking Pox, which the Death Guard spread in their wake. The Heretic Astartes send Poxwalkers ahead of their advance in a tide of rotting flesh, using them to soak up the enemy's fusillades and artillery bombardments. Though slow and clumsy, these twisted creatures display a flicker of sentience that allows them to wield debris and battlefield detritus as makeshift weapons. They are also formidably resilient, continuing to stumble towards the enemy even when lasfire and explosions have shredded their flesh and spilled their foetid intestines. Most appalling of all is the cacophony of agonised groans made by a horde of Poxwalkers. Those unfortunate victims transformed into these abominations remain horribly aware of their plight, yet are unable to exercise any control over their form. Trapped forever within a cage of mouldering flesh, their howls of despair are horrifying indeed. Worse, the awful sound spreads a spiritual contagion to those who hear it, inflicting new hosts with the horror of the Walking Pox.

To follow the optional, additional steps on this page, you will require the paints shown below.

CITADEL DRY CHRONUS BLUE

CITADEL BASE LEADBELCHER

CITADEL SHADE NULN OIL

CITADEL BASE MEPHISTON RED

CITADEL BASE RAKARTH FLESH

EXTRA STEPS

INTERCESSORS

Using the painting techniques detailed earlier and the small selection of additional paints here, you can follow the straightforward steps below to take the simple paint job on your Primaris Space Marine Intercessors (pg 74) to the next level.

1

Apply a drybrush of Chronus Blue to the model's armour, being careful while doing so to avoid getting this colour on the metal or bolt rifle casing.

2

Now, using an M Base brush, carefully apply Leadbelcher to all the bare metal components on the Intercessor's bolt rifle, as shown in the image above.

5

For a last flourish, you can use Rakarth Flesh to highlight the parchment of your Intercessor's purity seal.

3

Once the metal areas are fully dried, apply a careful shade of Nuln Oil to the Intercessor's bolt rifle and the recesses of his power armour.

4

Lastly, using Mephiston Red and an S Layer brush, pick out the eye lenses of the Intercessor's helm, and the wax of his purity seal (if he has one).

78

PLAGUE MARINES

Once you have mastered the basic painting steps for your Death Guard Plague Marines, you may wish to follow up with these optional stages to lift their paint job and apply an extra level of gruesome detail that will really make them stand out on the battlefield.

To follow the optional, additional steps on this page, you will require the paints shown below.

CITADEL SHADE CARROBURG CRIMSON

CITADEL LAYER PALLID WYCH FLESH

CITADEL DRY NECRON COMPOUND

CITADEL BASE ABADDON BLACK

CITADEL BASE MOURNFANG BROWN

1

Using Carroburg Crimson, apply a careful shade to all the areas of mutated flesh on your model, such as the tentacle arm on this Plague Marine.

2

Once your shade is completely dry, use Pallid Wych Flesh to apply a drybrush to the model's mutated flesh and any bone areas.

3

Now take Necron Compound and apply a carefully targeted drybrush to the bronze and silver metals on the model.

4

Finally, use Abaddon Black to apply an even coat to the Plague Marine's bolter casing and the edge of his base.

5

As an extra touch you can, if you wish, paint any wooden areas such as the bolter grip here with Mournfang Brown.

READYING FOR WAR

The battle report on page 30 offers a glimpse of how exciting, tactically varied and action-packed the Warhammer 40,000 tabletop wargame is, and how simple it is to get started.

The rules on the following pages will give you everything you need to start playing. You'll find easy-to-read instructions for each phase of a typical game, as well as diagrams to give you a clear idea of how everything works. With these rules you can match whichever armies you wish against each other in an endless variety of exciting scenarios.

Now it's your turn to join in the fun! It couldn't be easier to jump into the battlefields of the far future – once you've assembled your models, all you need are some dice, a tape measure, and someone to play with. Sociable and endlessly enjoyable, wargaming is a wonderful way to spend an afternoon – or a day, if you're feeling particularly ambitious.

From here, the possibilities are limitless. Games Workshop has an ever-expanding range of supplements and expansions, each introducing unique settings Battlezone rules for the regions of the galaxy you're battling across or providing new ways to play. Whether you utilise these new missions, variations and campaigns, or simply draw inspiration from the rich tapestry of Warhammer 40,000 to create your own adventures, there really are no limits to the tales you can tell.

DATASHEETS

The warriors, monsters and war machines that fight for control of the galaxy are incredibly diverse, each with their own style of waging war. Each unit has a datasheet that lists the characteristics, wargear and abilities of the models in that unit – here we explain what some of it means, while the core rules (over the page) explain how it's all used in the game.

1. UNIT NAME

Models move and fight in units, which can have one or more models. Here you'll find the name of the unit.

2. BATTLEFIELD ROLE

This is typically used when making a Battle-forged army (see the *Warhammer 40,000* rulebook).

3. POWER RATING

The higher this is, the more powerful the unit! You can determine the Power Level of your entire army by adding up the Power Ratings of all the units in your army.

4. PROFILES

These contain the following characteristics that tell you how mighty the models in the unit are:

Move (M): This is the speed at which a model moves across the battlefield.

Weapon Skill (WS): This tells you a model's skill at hand-to-hand fighting. If a model has a Weapon Skill of '-' it is unable to fight in melee and cannot make close combat attacks at all.

Ballistic Skill (BS): This shows how accurate a model is when shooting with ranged weapons. If a model has a Ballistic Skill of '-' it has no proficiency with ranged weapons and cannot make shooting attacks at all.

Strength (S): This indicates how strong a model is and how likely it is to inflict damage in hand-to-hand combat.

Toughness (T): This reflects the model's resilience against physical harm.

Wounds (W): Wounds show how much damage a model can sustain before it succumbs to its injuries.

Attacks (A): This tells you how many times a model can strike blows in hand-to-hand combat.

Leadership (Ld): This reveals how courageous, determined or self-controlled a model is.

Save (Sv): This indicates the protection a model's armour gives.

5. UNIT COMPOSITION

This tells you what models are in the unit.

6. WARGEAR

This covers the basic weapons and equipment the models are armed with.

7. ABILITIES

Many units have exciting special abilities that are not covered by the core rules; these will be described here.

8. WEAPONS

The weapons that a unit comes equipped with are described using a set of characteristics as follows:

Range: How far the weapon can shoot. Weapons with a range of 'Melee' can only be used in hand-to-hand combat. All other weapons are referred to as ranged weapons.

Type: These are all explained under the Shooting and Fight phases of the core rules.

Strength (S): How likely the weapon is to inflict damage. If a weapon's Strength lists 'User', it is equal to the wielder's current Strength. If a weapon lists a modifier such as '+1' or 'x2', you should modify the user's current Strength characteristic as shown to determine the weapon's Strength. For example, if a weapon's Strength was 'x2', and the user had a Strength characteristic of 6, that weapon has Strength 12.

Armour Penetration (AP): How good it is at getting through armour.

Damage (D): The amount of damage inflicted by a successful hit.

Other weapons, for example those a unit may take as an optional choice, are typically described elsewhere, such as in a codex.

9. KEYWORDS

All datasheets have a list of keywords, sometimes separated into Faction keywords and other keywords. The former can be used as a guide to help decide which models to include in your army, but otherwise both sets of keywords are functionally the same. Sometimes a rule will say that it applies to models that have a specific keyword. For example, a rule might say that it applies to 'all **Adeptus Astartes** models'. This means it would only apply to models that have the Adeptus Astartes keyword on their datasheet.

TYRANID WARRIORS

NAME	M	WS	BS	S	T	W	A	Ld	Sv
Tyranid Warrior	6"	3+	4+	4	4	3	3	9	4+

This unit contains 3 Tyranid Warriors. It can include up to 3 additional Tyranid Warriors (**Power Rating +5**) or up to 6 additional Tyranid Warriors (**Power Rating +10**). Each model is armed with a pair of scything talons and a devourer.

WEAPON	RANGE	TYPE	S	AP	D	ABILITIES
Devourer	18"	Assault 3	4	0	1	This weapon can be fired within 1" of an enemy unit, and can target enemy units within 1" of friendly units.
Flesh hooks	6"	Assault 2	User	0	1	You can re-roll hit rolls of 1 when attacking with this weapon. If the bearer has more than one pair of scything talons, it can make 1 additional attack with this weapon

② ④ ③ ①

WARBOSS

⑤ ⑥

NAME	M	WS	BS	S	T	W	A	Ld	Sv
Warboss	5"	2+	5+	6	5	6	4	8	4+

④

A Warboss is a single model armed with a kustom shoota, a big choppa and stikkbombs.

⑧

WEAPON	RANGE	TYPE	S	AP	D	ABILITIES
Kustom shoota	18"	Assault 4	4	0	1	-
Attack squig	Melee	Melee	4	-1	1	Each time a model with an attack squig fights, it can make 2 additional attacks with this weapon.
Big choppa	Melee	Melee	+2	-1	2	-
Stikkbomb	6"	Grenade D6	3	0	1	-

WARGEAR OPTIONS
- This model may replace its kustom shoota with one item from the *Shooty Weapons* or *Choppy Weapons* lists.
- This model may replace its big choppa with one item from the *Choppy Weapons* list.
- This model may take an attack squig.

ABILITIES   'Ere We Go, Mob Rule (pg 10)

⑦   **Waaagh!:** Friendly **ORK INFANTRY** units within 6" of this model at the start of the Charge phase can charge even if they Advanced this turn.

Breakin' Heads: If a <CLAN> unit fails a Morale test within 3" of a friendly <CLAN> WARBOSS, they can restore order with a brutal display of violence. If they do, the unit suffers D3 mortal wounds but the Morale test is then considered to have been passed.

FACTION KEYWORDS	ORK, <CLAN>
⑨ **KEYWORDS**	CHARACTER, INFANTRY, WARBOSS

WARHAMMER 40,000 CODEXES

So now you know what a datasheet is and how it works – in conjunction with the core rules that follow (plus your Citadel Miniatures, battlefield, dice and tape measure, of course!), you've got everything you need to start playing games of Warhammer 40,000 and dive into epic battle.

But where do you find datasheets? Well, when you buy a box of Citadel Miniatures they'll be in the box with them, and they are also present in codexes. A codex is the ultimate resource for your chosen army (or armies!), containing datasheets for all the miniatures that are part of a particular Faction. But that's not all – in codexes you'll also find army-specific special rules that reflect the character of the army, exciting Warlord Traits, Stratagems, wargear, and even unique relics.

Each codex is also filled with a wealth of inspirational background material, organisational information, stunning art and miniatures photography, colour guides and heraldry, all of which provide context for how a Faction works in the Warhammer 40,000 universe. Head over to games-workshop.com to find out more.

MODIFYING CHARACTERISTICS

Some large models' characteristics can change as the model suffers damage – look at such a model's remaining wounds and consult the appropriate row of the chart on their datasheet to determine its current characteristics.

You may also encounter abilities and rules that modify a characteristic. All modifiers are cumulative, though you should apply any multiplication or division to the characteristic (rounding fractions up) before applying any addition or subtraction.

You may encounter a characteristic that is a random value instead of a number. For example, a Move characteristic might be 2D6", or an Attacks value might be D6. When a unit with a random Move characteristic is selected to move, determine the entire unit's move distance by rolling the indicated number of dice (pg 86). For all other characteristics, roll to determine the value on an individual – per-model – basis each time the unit makes attacks, inflicts damage, and so on. Note that, regardless of the source, characteristics of '-' can never be modified, and the Strength, Toughness and Leadership characteristics of a model can never be modified below 1.

WARHAMMER 40,000

CODEX ADEPTUS ASTARTES
GREY KNIGHTS

CORE RULES

Warhammer 40,000 puts you in command of a force of mighty warriors and war machines. The core rules on these pages contain everything you need to know in order to use your Citadel Miniatures collection to wage glorious battle across the war-torn galaxy.

TOOLS OF WAR

In order to fight a battle, you will require a tape measure and some dice.

Distances in Warhammer 40,000 are measured in inches (") between the closest points of the bases of the models you're measuring to and from. If a model does not have a base, such is the case with many vehicles, measure to and from the closest point of that model's hull instead. You can measure distances whenever you wish.

Warhammer 40,000 uses six-sided dice, sometimes abbreviated to D6. Some rules refer to 2D6, 3D6 and so on – in such cases, roll that many D6s and add the results together. If a rule requires you to roll a D3, roll a dice and halve the total. When halving any dice roll, round fractions up before applying modifiers (if any) to the result. All modifiers are cumulative. If a rule requires a dice roll of, for example, 3 or more, this is often abbreviated to 3+.

MODELS & DATASHEETS

The rules and characteristics for all models, and some terrain features, are presented on datasheets, which you will need in order to use the models in battle.

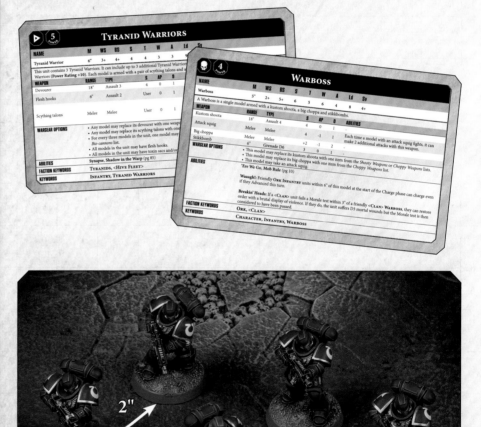

UNITS

Models move and fight in units, made up of one or more models. A unit must be set up and finish any sort of move as a group, with every model within 2" horizontally, and 6" vertically, of at least one other model from their unit: this is called unit coherency. If anything causes a unit to become split up during a battle, it must re-establish its unit coherency the next time it moves.

THE BATTLE ROUND

Warhammer 40,000 is played in a series of battle rounds. During each battle round, both players have a turn. The same player always takes the first turn in each battle round – the mission you are playing will tell you which player this is. Each turn consists of a series of phases, which must be resolved in order. The phases are as follows:

1 MOVEMENT PHASE
Move any units that are capable of doing so.

2 PSYCHIC PHASE
Psykers can use powerful mental abilities.

3 SHOOTING PHASE
Your units may shoot enemy units.

4 CHARGE PHASE
Your units may move into close combat against enemy units.

5 FIGHT PHASE
Both players' units pile in and attack with melee weapons.

6 MORALE PHASE
Test the courage of depleted units.

Once a player's turn has ended, their opponent then starts their turn. Once both players have completed a turn, the battle round has been completed and the next one begins, and so on, until the battle is concluded.

1 MOVEMENT PHASE

The ground shakes to the tread of marching feet and the growl of engines as armies advance across the battlefield and vie for advantageous positions.

Start your Movement phase by picking one of your units and moving each model in that unit until you've moved all the models you want to. You can then pick another unit to move, until you have moved as many of your units as you wish. No model can be moved more than once in each Movement phase.

2. PSYCHIC PHASE

3. SHOOTING PHASE

4. CHARGE PHASE

5. FIGHT PHASE

6. MORALE PHASE

MOVING

A model can be moved in any direction, to a distance, in inches, equal to or less than the Move characteristic on its datasheet. No part of the model's base (or hull) can move further than this. It cannot be moved through other models or through terrain features such as walls, but can be moved vertically in order to climb or traverse any scenery.

If the datasheet for a model says it can **FLY**, it can move across models and terrain as if they were not there.

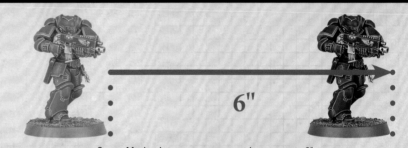

6"

Space Marine Intercessors can each move up to 6".

Ⓐ

1. The Death Guard player starts by moving their unit of Plague Marines Ⓐ . They have a Move characteristic of 5", and so are moved as close as possible towards the Space Marines.

The Death Guard player then moves their Malignant Plaguecaster Ⓑ , and decides this model should Advance...

MINIMUM MOVE

Some models that can **FLY** have a Move characteristic consisting of two values. The first is the model's minimum speed – in the Movement phase, all parts of the model's base must end the move at least that far from where they started. The second is its maximum speed – no part of the model's base can be moved further than this. If a model cannot make its minimum move, or is forced to move off the battlefield because of its minimum speed, it is destroyed and removed from the battlefield – the model has either stalled and crashed or been forced to abandon the battle.

ENEMY MODELS

All models in the same army are friendly models. Models controlled by an opposing player are enemy models. When you move a model in the Movement phase, it may not be moved within 1" of any enemy models.

FALLING BACK

Units starting the Movement phase within 1" of an enemy unit can either remain stationary or Fall Back. If you choose to Fall Back, the unit must end its move more than 1" away from all enemy units. If a unit Falls Back, it cannot Advance (see below), or charge (pg 96) later that turn. A unit that Falls Back also cannot shoot later that turn unless it can **FLY**.

ADVANCING

When you pick a unit to move in the Movement phase, you can declare that it will Advance. Roll a dice and add the result to the Move characteristics of all models in the unit for that Movement phase. A unit that Advances can't shoot or charge later that turn.

WOBBLY MODEL SYNDROME

Sometimes you may find that a particular piece of terrain makes it hard to put a model exactly where you want. If you delicately balance it in place, it is very likely to fall as soon as somebody nudges the table, leaving your painted model damaged or even broken. In cases like this, we find it is perfectly acceptable to leave the model in a safer position, as long as both players have agreed and know its 'actual' location. If, later on, your enemy is considering shooting the model, you will have to hold it back in the proper place so they can check if it is visible.

REINFORCEMENTS

Many units have the ability to be set up on the battlefield mid-turn, sometimes by using teleporters, grav chutes or other, more esoteric means. Typically, this happens at the end of the Movement phase, but it can also happen during other phases. Units that are set up in this manner cannot move or Advance further during the turn they arrive – their entire Movement phase is used in deploying to the battlefield – but they can otherwise act normally (shoot, charge, etc.) for the rest of their turn. Units that arrive as reinforcements count as having moved in their Movement phase for all rules purposes, such as shooting Heavy weapons (pg 94). Any unit that has not arrived on the battlefield by the end of the battle counts as having been destroyed.

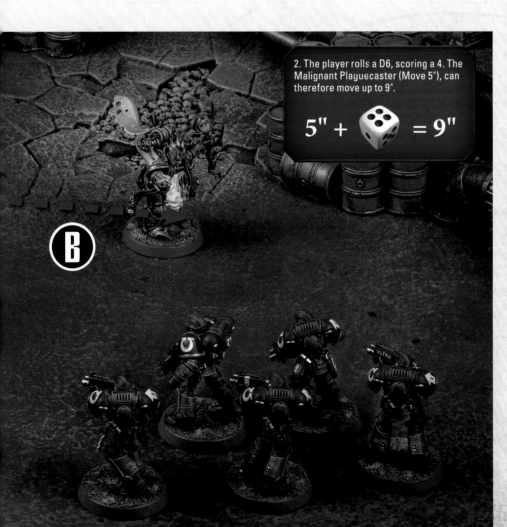

2. The player rolls a D6, scoring a 4. The Malignant Plaguecaster (Move 5"), can therefore move up to 9".

$$5" + \text{⚃} = 9"$$

1. MOVEMENT PHASE

2 PSYCHIC PHASE

Warrior mystics and sorcerers wield the strange power of the warp to aid their allies and destroy their foes. Harnessing this force is not without risk, however, and with the smallest mistake, the effort can spell doom for all nearby.

3. SHOOTING PHASE

4. CHARGE PHASE

5. FIGHT PHASE

6. MORALE PHASE

PSYCHIC SEQUENCE

1. Choose psyker and power
2. Make Psychic test
3. Enemy takes Deny the Witch test
4. Resolve psychic power

1. CHOOSE PSYKER & POWER

Some models are noted as being a **PSYKER** on their datasheet. Psykers can manifest their otherworldly abilities and attempt to deny enemy sorceries. The powers a psyker knows, and the number of powers they can attempt to manifest or deny each Psychic phase, are detailed on their datasheet.

PSYCHIC POWERS

Unless stated otherwise, all psykers know the *Smite* psychic power, listed below. Some know other powers instead of, or in addition to, *Smite* – the model's datasheets and other supplementary rules you are using will make it clear which powers each psyker knows. If a psyker generates their powers before the battle, do so immediately before either player starts to deploy their army.

SMITE

Smite has a warp charge value of 5. If manifested, the closest visible enemy unit within 18" of the psyker suffers D3 mortal wounds (pg 95). If the result of the Psychic test was more than 10, the target suffers D6 mortal wounds instead.

1. The Death Guard player only has a single psyker – the Malignant Plaguecaster **A**. This model attempts to manifest the *Smite* power.

2. MAKE PSYCHIC TEST

A psyker can attempt to manifest a psychic power they know by taking a Psychic test. To do so, roll 2D6. If the total is equal to or greater than that power's warp charge value, the power is successfully manifested. A psyker cannot attempt to manifest the same psychic power more than once in a turn.

PERILS OF THE WARP

If you roll a double 1 or a double 6 when taking a Psychic test, the psyker immediately suffers Perils of the Warp. The psyker suffers D3 mortal wounds as the forces of the Daemon-haunted warp claw at their mind. If the psyker is slain by Perils of the Warp, the power they were attempting to manifest automatically fails and each unit within 6" immediately suffers D3 mortal wounds, as the psyker is dragged into the warp or else detonates in a burst of empyric feedback.

3. DENY THE WITCH TESTS

A psyker can attempt to resist a psychic power that has been manifested by an enemy model within 24" by taking a Deny the Witch test – this takes place immediately, even though it is not your turn. To do so, roll 2D6. If the total is greater than the result of the Psychic test that manifested the power, it has been resisted and its effects are negated. Only one attempt to deny each successfully manifested psychic power can be made each turn, regardless of the number of psykers you have within 24" of the enemy model manifesting the psychic power.

4. RESOLVE PSYCHIC POWER

So long as the Psychic test was successful, the psyker did not die as a result of the Perils of the Warp, and the attempt was not thwarted by a Deny the Witch test, then you may resolve the effect of the psychic power, which will be described in the power itself.

RE-ROLLS

Some rules allow you to re-roll a dice roll, which means you get to roll some or all of the dice again. You can never re-roll a dice more than once, and re-rolls happen before modifiers (if any) are applied.

ROLL-OFFS

Some rules instruct players to roll off. To do so, both players roll a D6, and whoever scores highest wins the roll-off. In the case of a tie, both players re-roll their D6; this is the only time players can re-roll a re-roll – if the second and subsequent rolls are also tied, keep on rolling until a winner is decided.

SEQUENCING

While playing Warhammer 40,000, you'll occasionally find that two or more rules are to be resolved at the same time – normally 'at the start of the Movement phase' or 'before the battle begins'. When this happens during the game, the player whose turn it is chooses the order. If these things occur before or after the game, or at the start or end of a battle round, the players roll off and the winner decides in what order the rules are resolved.

2. The Death Guard player takes a Psychic test by rolling 2D6, and scores a total of 6. This is greater than the power's warp charge value of 5, so the test is passed.

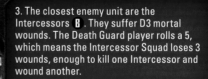

3. The closest enemy unit are the Intercessors **B**. They suffer D3 mortal wounds. The Death Guard player rolls a 5, which means the Intercessor Squad loses 3 wounds, enough to kill one Intercessor and wound another.

÷ 2 rounds to 3

1. MOVEMENT PHASE

2. PSYCHIC PHASE

3 SHOOTING PHASE

Guns thunder and shrapnel falls from the sky. Muzzle flare shines through the gloom in bursts, beams of las-fire illuminate the fog of war, and spent ammunition cartridges and power cells are left discarded across the battlefield.

4. CHARGE PHASE

5. FIGHT PHASE

6. MORALE PHASE

SHOOTING SEQUENCE

1. Choose unit to shoot with
2. Choose targets
3. Choose ranged weapon
4. Resolve attacks
   - Make hit roll
   - Make wound roll
   - Enemy allocates wound
   - Enemy makes saving throw
   - Inflict damage

CHARACTERS

Some models are noted as being a **CHARACTER** on their datasheet. These heroes, officers, prophets and warlords are powerful individuals that can have a great impact on the course of a battle. The swirling maelstrom of the battlefield can make it difficult to pick out such individuals as targets, however. A **CHARACTER** can only be chosen as a target in the Shooting phase if they are the closest visible enemy unit to the model that is shooting. This does not apply to **CHARACTERS** with a Wounds characteristic of 10 or more, due to their sheer size.

1. The Death Guard player selects the unit of Plague Marines **A** to shoot with. The Plague Marines will shoot with their boltguns, while the Plague Champion will throw a krak grenade.

2. The targets **B** are 6" away, which is within range of the Plague Marines' **boltguns** ——▶. These are Rapid Fire 1 weapons, and so each fires twice at half range or less. The Death Guard player therefore rolls 8 dice to see if the shots hit. The Plague Marines' Ballistic Skill is 3+, so 6 shots hit and the others miss.

3. The Death Guard player then makes a wound roll for each hit. A **boltgun's** Strength of 4 equals the target's Toughness of 4, meaning a roll of 4+ is required to successfully wound the target. The Death Guard player rolls for each shot, four of which are successful. The Space Marine player will now need to make a saving throw for each.

1. CHOOSE UNIT TO SHOOT WITH

In your Shooting phase you can shoot with models armed with ranged weapons. First, you must pick one of your units to shoot with. You may not pick a unit that Advanced or Fell Back this turn, or a unit that is within 1" of an enemy unit. Unless otherwise stated, each model in the unit attacks with all of the ranged weapons it is armed with. After all of the unit's models have fired, you can choose another unit to shoot with, until all eligible units that you want to shoot with have done so.

2. CHOOSE TARGETS

Having chosen a shooting unit, you must pick the target unit, or units, for the attacks. In order to target an enemy unit, a model from that unit must be within the Range of the weapon being used (as listed on its profile) and be visible to the shooting model. If unsure, stoop down and get a look from behind the shooting model to see if any part of the target is visible. For the purposes of determining visibility, a model can see through other models in its own unit.

Models cannot target enemy units that are within 1" of friendly models – the risk of hitting your own troops is too great.

3. CHOOSE RANGED WEAPON

The weapons a model has are listed on its datasheet. If a model has several weapons, it can shoot all of them at the same target, or it can shoot each at a different enemy unit. Similarly, if a unit contains more than one model, they can shoot at the same, or different targets as you choose. In either case, declare how you will split the shooting unit's shots before any dice are rolled, and resolve all the shots against one target before moving on to the next.

NUMBER OF ATTACKS

Each time a model shoots a ranged weapon, it will make a number of attacks. You roll one dice for each attack being made. The number of attacks a model can make with a weapon, and therefore the number of dice you can roll, is found on the weapon's profile, along with the weapon's type. A weapon's type can impact the number of attacks it can make (see overleaf).

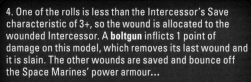

4. One of the rolls is less than the Intercessor's Save characteristic of 3+, so the wound is allocated to the wounded Intercessor. A **boltgun** inflicts 1 point of damage on this model, which removes its last wound and it is slain. The other wounds are saved and bounce off the Space Marines' power armour...

Ⓐ

Ⓑ

WEAPON TYPES

There are five types of ranged weapon: Assault, Heavy, Rapid Fire, Grenade and Pistol. A model shooting one of these weapons can make a number of attacks equal to the number written on its profile after its type. For example, a model firing an 'Assault 1' weapon can make 1 attack with that weapon; a model firing a 'Heavy 3' weapon can make 3 attacks, etc.

If a weapon has more than one attack, it must make all of its attacks against the same target unit.

Each type of ranged weapon also has an additional rule that, depending upon the situation, might affect the accuracy of the weapon or when it can be fired. These are as follows:

ASSAULT

Assault weapons fire so rapidly or indiscriminately that they can be shot from the hip as warriors dash forwards into combat.

A model with an Assault weapon can fire it even if it Advanced earlier that turn. If it does so, you must subtract 1 from any hit rolls made when firing that weapon this turn.

HEAVY

Heavy weapons are the biggest and deadliest guns on the battlefield, but require reloading, careful set-up or bracing to fire at full effect.

If a model with a Heavy weapon moved in its preceding Movement phase, you must subtract 1 from any hit rolls made when firing that weapon this turn.

RAPID FIRE

Rapid Fire weapons are versatile weapons capable of aimed single shots at long range or controlled bursts of fire at close quarters.

A model firing a Rapid Fire weapon doubles the number of attacks it makes if its target is within half the weapon's maximum range.

GRENADE

Grenades are handheld explosive devices that a warrior throws at the enemy while their squad mates provide covering fire.

Each time a unit shoots, a single model in the unit that is equipped with Grenades may throw one instead of firing any other weapon.

PISTOL

Pistols are carried one-handed and can even be used in a melee to shoot at point-blank range. Many warriors carry one as a sidearm, alongside their primary weapon.

A model can fire a Pistol even if there are enemy units within 1" of its own unit, but it must target the closest enemy unit. In such circumstances, the model can shoot its Pistol even if other friendly units are within 1" of the same enemy unit.

Each time a model equipped with both a Pistol and another type of ranged weapon (e.g. a Pistol and a Rapid Fire weapon) shoots, it can either shoot with its Pistol(s) or with all of its other weapons. Choose which it will fire (Pistols or non-Pistols) before making hit rolls.

6. A **krak grenade** inflicts D3 damage; the Death Guard player rolls a 6, inflicting 3 points of damage. This causes an Intercessor to lose both its wounds. As it is slain by this attack, the other point of damage is discarded and has no effect.

÷ 2 = 3

...5. The Plague Champion then throws a **krak grenade**, which hits. This grenade has a Strength of 6, which wounds the Intercessors on a roll of 3+ as its Strength is greater than the Intercessors' Toughness. The Space Marine player then rolls a 3 for their saving throw, but must subtract 1 from the roll because the krak grenade has an AP characteristic of -1. The final result of 2 fails to protect the Space Marines.

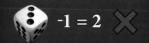 -1 = 2 ✗

4. RESOLVE ATTACKS

Attacks can be made one at a time, or, in some cases, you can roll for multiple attacks together. The following sequence is used to make attacks one at a time:

1. **Hit Roll:** Each time a model makes an attack, roll a dice. If the roll is equal to or greater than the attacking model's Ballistic Skill characteristic, then it scores a hit with the weapon it is using. If not, the attack fails and the attack sequence ends. A roll of 1 always fails, irrespective of any modifiers that may apply.

2. **Wound Roll:** If an attack scores a hit, you will then need to roll another dice to see if the attack successfully wounds the target. The roll required is determined by comparing the attacking weapon's Strength characteristic with the target's Toughness characteristic, as shown on the following table:

WOUND ROLL	
ATTACK'S STRENGTH VS TARGET'S TOUGHNESS	**D6 ROLL REQUIRED**
Is the Strength TWICE (or more) than the Toughness?	2+
Is the Strength GREATER than the Toughness?	3+
Is the Strength EQUAL to the Toughness?	4+
Is the Strength LOWER than the Toughness?	5+
Is the Strength HALF (or less) than the Toughness?	6+

If the roll is less than the required number, the attack fails and the attack sequence ends. A roll of 1 always fails, irrespective of any modifiers that may apply.

3. **Allocate Wound:** If an attack successfully wounds the target, the player commanding the target unit allocates the wound to any model in the unit (the chosen model does not have to be within range or visible to the attacking unit). If a model in the target unit has already lost any wounds, the damage must be allocated to that model.

4. **Saving Throw:** The player commanding the target unit then makes a saving throw by rolling a dice and modifying the roll by the Armour Penetration characteristic of the weapon that caused the damage. For example, if the weapon has an Armour Penetration of -1, then 1 is subtracted from the saving throw roll. If the result is equal to, or greater than, the Save characteristic of the model the wound was allocated to, then the damage is prevented and the attack sequence ends. If the result is less than the model's Save characteristic, then the saving throw fails and the model suffers damage. A roll of 1 always fails, irrespective of any modifiers that may apply.

5. **Inflict Damage:** The damage inflicted is equal to the Damage characteristic of the weapon used in the attack. A model loses one wound for each point of damage it suffers. If a model's wounds are reduced to 0, it is either slain or destroyed and removed from play. If a model loses several wounds from a single attack and is destroyed, any excess damage inflicted by that attack is lost and has no effect.

THE MOST IMPORTANT RULE

In a game as detailed and wide-ranging as Warhammer 40,000, there may be times when you are not sure exactly how to resolve a situation that has come up during play. When this happens, have a quick chat with your opponent and apply the solution that makes the most sense to both of you (or seems the most fun!). If no single solution presents itself, you and your opponent should roll off, and whoever rolls highest gets to choose what happens. Then you can get on with the fighting!

TERRAIN AND COVER

The battlefields of the far future are littered with terrain features such as ruins, craters and twisted copses. Models can take shelter within such terrain features to gain protection against incoming weapons' fire.

If a unit is entirely on or within any terrain feature, add 1 to its models' saving throws against shooting attacks to represent the cover received from the terrain (invulnerable saves are unaffected). Units gain no benefit from cover in the Fight phase (pg 98).

MORTAL WOUNDS

Some attacks inflict mortal wounds – these are so powerful that no armour or force field can withstand their fury. Each mortal wound inflicts one point of damage on the target unit. Do not make a wound roll or saving throw (including invulnerable saves) against a mortal wound – just allocate it as you would any other wound and inflict damage to a model in the target unit as described above. Unlike normal attacks, excess damage from attacks that inflict mortal wounds is not lost. Instead keep allocating damage to another model in the target unit until either all the damage has been allocated or the target unit is destroyed.

INVULNERABLE SAVES

Some models possess supernatural reflexes or are protected by force fields that grant them an invulnerable save. Each time a wound is allocated to a model with an invulnerable save, you can choose to use either its normal Save characteristic or its invulnerable save, but not both. If a model has more than one invulnerable save, it can only use one of them – choose which it will use. If you use a model's invulnerable save, it is never modified by a weapon's Armour Penetration value.

1. MOVEMENT PHASE

2. PSYCHIC PHASE

3. SHOOTING PHASE

4 CHARGE PHASE

Warriors hurl themselves into battle to slay with blade, hammer and claw.

5. FIGHT PHASE

6. MORALE PHASE

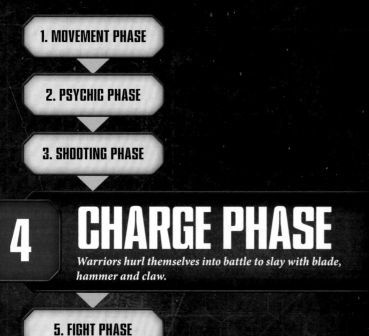

CHARGE SEQUENCE

1. Choose unit to charge with
2. Choose targets
3. Enemy resolves Overwatch
4. Roll 2D6 and make charge move

1. CHOOSE UNIT TO CHARGE WITH

Any of your units within 12" of the enemy in your Charge phase can make a charge move. You may not choose a unit that Advanced or Fell Back this turn, nor one that started the Charge phase within 1" of an enemy.

1. The Death Guard player chooses the Plague Marines **A** to charge the Intercessors **B** .

2. The Space Marine player fires Overwatch and makes 4 hit rolls. Models only hit on 6s when firing Overwatch, however both hits go on to wound, and then both saving throws are failed – two models are slain!

2. CHOOSE TARGETS

Once you have chosen an eligible unit, select one or more enemy units within 12" of them as the target(s) of the charge. Each target unit can then attempt to fire Overwatch.

3. OVERWATCH

Each time a charge is declared against a unit, the target unit can immediately fire Overwatch at the would-be attacker. A target unit can potentially fire Overwatch several times a turn, though it cannot fire if there are any enemy models within 1" of it. Overwatch is resolved like a normal shooting attack (albeit one resolved in the enemy's Charge phase) and uses all the normal rules except that a 6 is always required for a successful hit roll, irrespective of the firing model's Ballistic Skill or any modifiers.

4. MAKE CHARGE MOVE

After any Overwatch has been resolved, roll 2D6. Each model in the charging unit can move up to this number of inches – this is their charge distance this turn. The first model you move must finish within 1" of an enemy model from one of the target units. No models in the charging unit can move within 1" of an enemy unit that was not a target of its charge. If this is impossible, the charge fails and no models in the charging unit move this phase. Once you've moved all the models in the charging unit, choose another eligible unit and repeat the above procedure until all eligible units that you want to make charge moves have done so. No unit can be selected to charge more than once in each Charge phase.

HEROIC INTERVENTION

After the enemy has completed all of their charge moves, any of your **CHARACTERS** that are within 3" of an enemy unit may perform a Heroic Intervention. Any that do so can move up to 3", so long as they end the move closer to the nearest enemy model.

3. After resolving Overwatch, the Death Guard player rolls 2D6, scoring 7. The Plague Marines can charge 7" – enough to move within 1" of the Intercessors.

⚅ + ⚄ =7

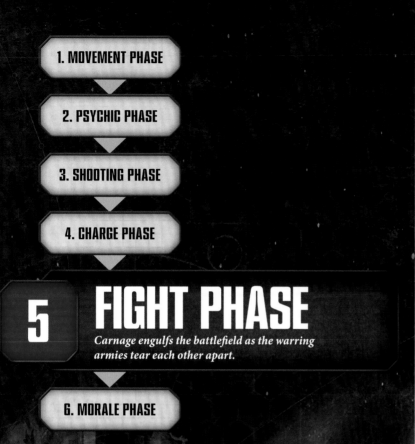

1. MOVEMENT PHASE

2. PSYCHIC PHASE

3. SHOOTING PHASE

4. CHARGE PHASE

5 FIGHT PHASE

Carnage engulfs the battlefield as the warring armies tear each other apart.

6. MORALE PHASE

1. Units that charged always resolve their fights first. In this case, that means the Plague Marines unit fights first.

2. They start by piling in, each model moving up to 3" closer to the nearest model. All are now within 1" of an enemy.

FIGHT SEQUENCE

1. Choose unit to fight with
2. Pile in up to 3"
3. Choose targets
4. Choose melee weapon
5. Resolve close combat attacks
   - Make hit roll
   - Make wound roll
   - Enemy allocates wound
   - Enemy makes saving throw
   - Inflict damage
6. Consolidate up to 3"

1. CHOOSE UNIT TO FIGHT WITH

Any unit that charged or has models within 1" of an enemy unit can be chosen to fight in the Fight phase. This includes all units, not just those controlled by the player whose turn it is. All units that charged this turn fight first. The player whose turn it is picks the order in which these units fight. After all charging units have fought, the players alternate choosing eligible units to fight with (starting with the player whose turn it is) until all eligible units on both sides have fought once each. No unit can be selected to fight more than once in each Fight phase. If one player runs out of eligible units, the other player completes all of their remaining fights, one unit after another. A fight is resolved in the following steps:

3. The Plague Marines will use their plague knives to make their close combat attacks against the Intercessor unit, but the Plague Champion, who has an Attacks characteristic of 2, chooses to make 1 close combat attack using his plague sword, and 1 using his power fist. The Death Guard player rolls 2 hit rolls for the plague knives (rolling a 3 and a 5), 1 for the plague sword (rolling a 3), and 1 for the power fist (rolling a 2).

Plague sword   Power fist

The Plague Marines and the Plague Champion both have a Weapon Skill characteristic of 3+, so the attack made with the power fist misses, but all the others hit. After wound rolls and saving throws are taken, another Intercessor has been slain. The Plague Marine unit then consolidates ▶ ▶ ▶ ▶, one of its models moving closer to the nearest enemy model.

2. PILE IN

You may move each model in the unit up to 3" – this move can be in any direction so long as the model ends the move closer to the nearest enemy model.

3. CHOOSE TARGETS

First, you must pick the target unit, or units, for the attacks. To target an enemy unit, the attacking model must either be within 1" of that unit, or within 1" of another model from its own unit that is itself within 1" of that enemy unit. This represents the unit fighting in two ranks. Models that charged this turn can only target enemy units that they charged in the previous phase.

If a model can make more than one close combat attack (see below), it can split them between eligible target units as you wish. Similarly if a unit contains more than one model, each can target a different enemy unit. In either case, declare how you will split the unit's close combat attacks before any dice are rolled, and resolve all attacks against one target before moving on to the next.

NUMBER OF ATTACKS

The number of close combat attacks a model makes against its target is determined by its Attacks characteristic. You roll one dice for each close combat attack being made. For example, if a model has an Attacks characteristic of 2, it can make 2 close combat attacks and you can therefore roll 2 dice.

4. CHOOSE MELEE WEAPON

Each time a model makes a close combat attack, it uses a melee weapon – the weapons a model is equipped with are described on its datasheet. If a datasheet does not list any melee weapons, the model is assumed to fight with a close combat weapon, which has the following profile:

WEAPON	RANGE	TYPE	S	AP	D
Close combat weapon	Melee	Melee	User	-	1

If a model has more than one melee weapon, choose which it will use before rolling the dice. If a model has more than one melee weapon and can make several close combat attacks, it can split its attacks between these weapons however you wish – declare how you will divide the attacks before any dice are rolled.

5. RESOLVE CLOSE COMBAT ATTACKS

Close combat attacks can be made one at a time, or in some cases you can roll the dice for a number of attacks together. The attack sequence for making close combat attacks is identical to that used for shooting attacks (pg 95) except you use the model's Weapon Skill characteristic instead of its Ballistic Skill to make hit rolls.

6. CONSOLIDATE

You may move each model in the unit up to 3" – this move can be in any direction so long as the model ends the move closer to the nearest enemy model.

The Death Guard player has no other units that can fight, so the Space Marine unit fights, slaying a single Plague Marine in return.

1. MOVEMENT PHASE

2. PSYCHIC PHASE

3. SHOOTING PHASE

4. CHARGE PHASE

5. FIGHT PHASE

In the Morale phase, starting with the player whose turn it is, players must take Morale tests for units from their army that have had models slain during the turn.

To take a Morale test, roll a dice and add the number of models from the unit that have been slain this turn. If the result of the Morale test exceeds the highest Leadership characteristic in the unit, the test is failed. For each point that the test is failed by, one model in that unit must flee and is removed from play. You choose which models flee from the units you command.

6 MORALE PHASE

Even the bravest heart may quail when the horrors of battle take their toll.

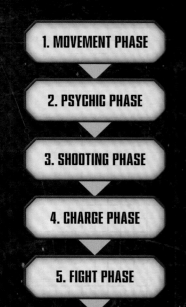

Both the Plague Marine unit and the Intercessors have suffered casualties during the turn, and so both have to take a Morale test.

The Death Guard player goes first, rolling a 6. Three Plague Marines died this turn, so 3 is added to the roll, for a total of 9. This exceeds the highest Leadership in the unit by 1 (the Plague Champion has a Leadership characteristic of 8), so 1 of the remaining models flees the battlefield.

The Space Marine player then takes a Morale test for the Intercessors, rolling a 3. When the number of casualties is added they have a total of 7. This is less than the unit's highest Leadership of 8 – the test is passed and no models flee.

The Death Guard turn is now complete, and the Space Marine player can now start their turn.

TRANSPORTS

Some models are noted as being a **TRANSPORT** on their datasheet – these vehicles ferry warriors to the front line, providing them with speed and protection. The following rules describe how units can embark and disembark from transports, and how they are used to move their passengers across the battlefield. Note that a unit cannot both embark and disembark in the same turn.

Transport Capacity: All transports have a transport capacity listed on their datasheet. This determines how many friendly models, and of what type, they can carry. A model's transport capacity can never be exceeded.

When you set up a transport, units can start the battle embarked within it instead of being set up separately – declare what units are embarked inside the transport when you set it up.

Embark: If all models in a unit end their move within 3" of a friendly transport, they can embark within it. Remove the unit from the battlefield and place it to one side – it is now embarked inside the transport.

Embarked units cannot normally do anything or be affected in any way whilst they are embarked. Unless specifically stated, abilities that affect other units within a certain range have no effect whilst the unit that has the ability is embarked.

If a transport is destroyed, any units embarked within it immediately disembark (see below) before the transport model is removed, but you must then roll one dice for each model you just set up on the battlefield. For each roll of 1, a model that disembarked (your choice) is slain.

Disembark: Any unit that begins its Movement phase embarked within a transport can disembark before the transport moves. When a unit disembarks, set it up on the battlefield so that all of its models are within 3" of the transport and not within 1" of any enemy models – any disembarking model that cannot be set up in this way is slain.

Units that disembark can then act normally (move, shoot, charge, fight, etc.) during the remainder of their turn. Note though, that even if you don't move disembarking units further in your Movement phase, they still count as having moved for any rules purposes, such as shooting Heavy weapons (pg 94).

FIGHTING A BATTLE

THE MISSION

Before you can wage war in a game of Warhammer 40,000, you must select a mission. The core rules include a single mission – Only War – which is ideal to get the action started quickly (see overleaf). Others can be found in other books, or you could play a mission of your own creation. If you and your opponent can't agree on which mission to play, both players should roll a dice, re-rolling ties, and whoever rolls the highest decides on the mission.

THE BATTLEFIELD

In the far future, battles are fought across an infinite variety of strange and alien planets where no land is left untouched by the blight of war. Crystal moons, derelict space hulks, carnivorous death worlds and nightmarish Daemon worlds are just a few of the fantastical landscapes that can be recreated whenever you play a game of Warhammer 40,000.

A battlefield can be any surface upon which the models can stand – a dining table, for example, or the floor. We typically assume a battlefield is 6' by 4' (although some missions will state other dimensions), but it should always be large enough to accommodate all your models – if it is not, simply increase the size of the battlefield.

Unless the mission you are playing instructs you otherwise, you should then feel free to create an exciting battlefield using any terrain features from your collection that you wish. In general, we recommend having one or two features in each 2' by 2' area. Don't worry if your battlefield doesn't match these requirements, but keep in mind that playing on very small or very large battlefields, or ones that are either a barren wasteland or filled to overflowing with terrain features, may give an advantage to one side or the other.

BATTLEZONES & EXPANSIONS

If you are battling in a specific battlezone, or if you are using a particular expansion, there might be additional rules pertaining to setting up the battlefield, and special rules that alter how some terrain interacts with your warriors. Bear these in mind when creating your battlefield.

THE WARLORD

Once you have mustered your army, nominate one of your models to be your Warlord.

If your Warlord is a CHARACTER, it can use a Warlord Trait – a preferred tactic or personal ability that marks them out amongst their peers. Immediately before either player starts to deploy their army, you can roll on the Warlord Trait table here to determine what Warlord Trait your Warlord has. Alternatively, choose the trait that most suits your Warlord's temperament or style of war.

WARLORD TRAITS

D3	WARLORD TRAIT
1	**Legendary Fighter:** If this Warlord charges in the Charge phase, add 1 to their Attacks characteristic until the end of the ensuing Fight phase.
2	**Inspiring Leader:** Friendly units within 6" of this Warlord can add 1 to their Leadership characteristic.
3	**Tenacious Survivor:** Roll a dice each time this Warlord loses a wound. On a 6, the Warlord shrugs off the damage and does not lose the wound.

ONLY WAR

The time has come to prove your worth as the greatest warlord in the galaxy! All that stands between you and ultimate glory is an enemy army bent upon your destruction.

THE ARMIES

In order to play this mission, you must first muster an army from the miniatures in your collection. You can include any models in your army.

Sometimes you may find that you do not have enough models to field a minimum-sized unit (this can be found on each unit's datasheet); if this is the case, you can still include one unit of that type in your army with as many models as you have available.

THE BATTLEFIELD

Create the battlefield and set up terrain. The players must then place objective markers to represent sites of tactical or strategic import that one or both armies are attempting to secure. Objective markers can be represented by any suitable marker or piece of terrain. Each player must place two objective markers anywhere on the battlefield, so long as they are each at least 10" away from any other objective marker. We suggest taking turns to place these, starting with whichever player wins a roll-off. A player controls an objective marker if there are more models from their army within 3" of it than there are enemy models (measure to the centre of the marker).

PRIMARY OBJECTIVES

Before setting up their armies, both players roll off. The player who rolls higher then rolls on the primary objectives table (see right) to determine which are used during the mission.

DEPLOYMENT

Once the victory conditions have been determined, the player who did not roll on the primary objectives table then divides the battlefield into two equal-sized halves. Their opponent then decides which half is their own deployment zone, and which half is the other player's deployment zone.

The players then alternate deploying their units, one at a time, starting with the player who did not pick their deployment zone. Models must be set up in their own deployment zone, more than 12" from the enemy deployment zone. Continue setting up units until both players have set up all the units in their army, or you have run out of room to set up more units.

POWER LEVEL

Before battle begins, determine each army's Power Level by adding together the Power Ratings of all the units set up in that army; whichever player has the lowest is the Underdog. If both have the same Power Level, the player who assigned the deployment zones is the Underdog.

If the difference between the Power Levels of the two armies is 10 to 19, the Underdog receives one Command re-roll; if the difference is 20 to 29, the Underdog receives two Command re-rolls, and so on. Each Command re-roll can be used once, at any point during the battle, to re-roll a single dice.

FIRST TURN

The Underdog chooses who has the first turn.

BATTLE LENGTH

The battle lasts for five battle rounds, or until one army has slain all of its foes.

VICTORY CONDITIONS

If one army has slain all of its foes, it immediately wins a major victory. Otherwise, at the end of the battle, the player who has the most victory points wins a major victory. If both players have the same number of victory points at the end of the battle, the Underdog wins a minor victory.

PRIMARY OBJECTIVES		
D3	**VICTORY CONDITIONS**	
1		**Slay and Secure:** At the end of the battle, each objective marker is worth 2 victory points to the player who controls it. Players also earn D3 victory points if the opposing army's Warlord was slain during the battle.
2		**Ancient Relic:** At the start of the first battle round, but before the first turn begins, randomly select one objective marker; remove the other objective markers from the battlefield. At the end of the battle, the remaining objective marker is worth 6 victory points to the player who controls it.
3		**Domination:** At the end of each turn, each objective marker is worth 1 victory point to the player who controls it. Keep a running score from turn to turn.

PRODUCED BY GAMES WORKSHOP IN NOTTINGHAM

Certain Citadel products may be dangerous if used incorrectly and Games Workshop does not recommend them for use by children under the age of 16 without adult supervision.

Whatever your age, be careful when using glues, bladed equipment and sprays and make sure that you read and follow the instructions on the packaging.

Games Workshop Ltd, Willow Rd, Lenton, Nottingham, NG7 2WS.

games-workshop.com